# AS/A-LEVEL
# Media Studies

David Probert

ESSENTIAL WORD
DICTIONARY

D0257372

Philip Allan Updates
Market Place
Deddington
Oxfordshire
OX15 0SE

Tel: 01869 338652
Fax: 01869 337590
e-mail: sales@philipallan.co.uk
www.philipallan.co.uk

ISBN-13: 978-0-86003-384-4
ISBN-10: 0-86003-384-8

Printed by Raithby, Lawrence & Co Ltd, Leicester

**Environmental information**
The paper on which this title is printed is sourced from managed, sustainable
forests.

P00515

# Introduction

This *Essential Word Dictionary* aims to provide you with invaluable definitions for AS and A2 Media Studies. Your media studies course will require you to discuss the technical, textual, cultural and institutional aspects of the various forms of media and the definitions in this dictionary cover all of these areas. Whether you are studying the processes of media production, the textual elements within a particular media product, the key personnel behind a television production, the audience profiles of our national newspapers or the organisations/companies behind film-making, the terms you need to know are listed in these pages.

For each of the terms in this dictionary, an initial definition is given followed by an extension of that definition. Those terms which are key concepts have been marked. There are also examples which will help to illustrate the meaning of the term. In many cases tips are included on applications of the term or issues you should be aware of in association with it. Throughout the dictionary there are cross-references to words and phrases defined elsewhere which are shown in this font.

Any essay or study which you write during your course will need to include specific media terms, used accurately and appropriately. Read the definitions in this dictionary carefully and check the examples given in order to make sure that the term is appropriate to the subject which you are analysing. One good test of this is to substitute your example for the ones listed in the definition and check that it fits the context.

This dictionary has been written to fulfil the criteria of AS and A2 Media Studies. It only contains terms which you might come across in the course of your studies at this level. Other media studies dictionaries are available, but many are aimed at an undergraduate market and therefore contain terms which you will not need. Use this dictionary to check your knowledge of terminology and to ensure that your essays are accurate and comprehensive.

**AA:** see Advertising Association.

**ABC:** see Audit Bureau of Circulation.

**ABC1 scale:** a system of social classification based on an individual's occupation, used by advertisers and market researchers:
- A professional workers — lawyers, doctors, managers of large organisations
- B shopkeepers, farmers, teachers, white-collar workers
- C1 skilled manual high grade — builders, carpenters, shop assistants, nurses
- C2 skilled manual low grade — electricians, plumbers
- D semi-skilled manual — bus drivers, lorry drivers, fitters
- E unskilled manual — general labourers, bartenders, porters
- ■ The scale is used to classify media audiences and in particular to distinguish between the readership of tabloid and quality circulations. It is also used by advertisers as one method of identifying audience profiles and different market segments.
- ■ *TIP* The system has drawbacks. It ignores the class people may think they belong to. In addition, social status does not necessarily relate to financial status, income, patterns of spending or aspirations.

**aberrant decoding:** see oppositional reading.

**Academy Awards (also known as 'the Oscars'):** awards presented annually in California to actors and film technicians by the Academy of Motion Picture Arts and Sciences, a film-industry organisation established in 1927 to promote film.
- ■ These awards are prestigious and subject to competitive lobbying by interested parties. They tend to be an endorsement of high-profile stars and big-budget films produced by US-dominated international film and media organisations.
- ■ The British Academy of Film and Television Arts awards, although less prestigious, tend to look more favourably on the British film industry.

**a**

**action code:** a narrative structure based on a dramatic sequence of events, often leading to a violent resolution.

■ The gangster film *Bonnie and Clyde* (Arthur Penn, 1967) follows an action code resolved by the death of the two protagonists in a hail of bullets in the closing moments of the film.

**active audience theory:** any of various theories of audience behaviour that see the audience as active participants in the process of decoding and making sense of media texts.

■ In active theories, the beliefs, values, social and educational background and life experiences audiences bring to a text are seen as influencing the way they accept, negotiate, or challenge the preferred reading. See Hall, Stuart.

■ *e.g.* encoding/decoding model, reception theory, uses and gratifications theory

**Actors' Equity Association:** the principal actors' trade union in Britain and the USA, founded to protect the interests of actors and performers. Actors can only be professionally employed if they hold an equity card and these can sometimes be difficult to obtain.

**actuality:** filming or reporting of real events as they occur.

■ *e.g.* filmed news reports

**Adobe Premiere:** a non-linear, video-editing computer software package used in colleges and schools.

■ Adobe Premiere allows the capturing, cropping and editing of video footage and is available on Macintosh and Windows platforms.

■ *TIP* When working in Adobe Premiere on a network with others, careful file management and the regular deletion of unwanted material is essential to avoid system crashes and to ensure efficient operation of the software. Saving material on the appropriate network drive and not just on an individual machine, together with the correct naming and identification of files, saves space and helps to avoid loss of files.

**adventure film:** a film genre in which the characters are placed in an exciting and often dangerous location far away from home.

■ Characters frequently face physical and environmental challenges, e.g. human enemies, dangerous or exotic animals, difficult terrain, natural disasters and dangerous missions.

■ Adventure films are usually produced as family entertainment with a range of characters to appeal to all ages, genders and ethnicities.

■ The genre is a broad one and includes action movies, historical fantasy films and even war movies.

■ *e.g.* *Time Bandits* (Terry Gilliam, 1981), *Spy Kids* (Robert Rodriguez, 2001), *Mission Impossible* (Brian De Palma, 1996)

**advertisement:** any paid-for communication designed to sell or publicise products or services.

**advertising:** media-led promotion of goods or services for sale whereby audiences are brought to the market and encouraged or persuaded to consume.

■ Through market research, audiences are identified and classified by class, gender, income, ethnicity, age, behaviour, attitudes, beliefs, values and patterns of consumption called lifestyles. Advertisers use market research to identify and classify audiences according to class, gender, income etc.

**advertising agency:** a company or firm engaged in the production of advertising and marketing materials in response to briefs developed with clients.

■ In a sophisticated media environment, advertising agencies play an important role in assessing the **attitudes, beliefs and values** of audiences and in relating campaigns to current social, cultural and political moods and trends.

■ Skilled and creative professional teams ensure that powerful and lasting images of products and their place in contemporary life are projected on audiences so that such images become part of their everyday cultural experience. The concept of a **brand** is crucial to successful advertising, and agencies concentrate on building brands in an increasingly competitive market.

■ *e.g.* Major worldwide agencies include: Ogilvy and Mather, J. Walter Thompson, McCann Erikson, BBDO Star Com, Mediavest, Midshare, OMD, Young and Rubicam Advertising, Bartle, Bogle, Hegarty and Saatchi and Saatchi.

■ *TIP* Some famous campaigns to research are: Levi jeans, Guinness, Volkswagen Beetle and Golf, Benetton, FCUK.

**Advertising Association (AA):** a UK federation of 32 trade bodies representing the advertising, promotional and marketing industries.

■ The Association acts as a pressure group and also develops and monitors standards within the industry through the process known as **self-regulation**.

■ Members include: the Cinema Advertising Association, the Institute of Practitioners in Advertising, ITV Network Ltd, the Royal Mail, the Market Research Society and the Newspaper Publishers Association.

**Advertising Standards Authority (ASA):** a body established by the Advertising Association in 1962 to oversee the self-regulation of the advertising industry.

■ Its code of advertising practice is a practical alternative to proposed restrictive government legislation.

■ The ASA publishes a monthly journal, passes judgement on issues relating to the content of advertisements and handles complaints brought to its attention by members of the public.

■ *e.g.* A recent television advertisement showing the course of life from birth to death was withdrawn after complaints that the birth scene was too graphic and might cause offence.

■ *TIP* Critics argue that the body was established by the advertising industry to protect its own interests rather than those of the general public.

**advertorial:** an advertisement in a newspaper or magazine presented as an editorial, thus attracting greater attention from readers who may not realise that it is paid for and therefore lacks objectivity.

■ *e.g.* Restaurants often disguise advertisements as reviews by food critics, which then appear as uncritical recommendations of the establishments concerned.

**Agence France-Presse (AFP):** a multimedia news agency delivering news and information to media organisations and governments worldwide.

■ With bureaus in 165 countries and 1,250 journalists, it produces around 700,000 words and 700 photos a day.

**agenda:** the order accorded to news or public-interest items in terms of media attention and coverage.

■ The higher a subject is placed on the agenda, the more media attention it receives and the greater the importance attached to the item by an audience. Subjects not on the media agenda and not reported attract a low level of public interest.

**agenda-setting:** the practice of determining what subjects are chosen for media coverage in such a way as to prioritise certain subjects at the expense of others.

■ This may be done by editors of newspapers or producers of television news programmes for personal, political or commercial reasons or in response to the perceived level of interest in a topic. It can lead to matters of public concern receiving little media coverage.

■ *e.g.* Owing to agenda-setting in the British tabloid press, the relationship between celebrities Victoria and David Beckham in 2004/05 received more prominent coverage than scientific reports on the progress of global warming.

**agitprop (short for 'Department of Agitation and Propaganda'):** an agency set up in the Soviet Union in 1920 to spread propaganda, especially in the then new medium of film.

■ The term is now used to describe any blatantly political propaganda.

**AKA:** journalistic shorthand for 'also known as'.

**alienation:** Marxist term for the emotional separation of workers from the product of their own labour as a result of complex mass-production processes.

■ Alienated workers have little pride in the products they help to create and have no sense of responsibility towards their employer. Work is merely a means of earning money. Personal gratification, identity and self-esteem are sought outside the workplace through social contact, for example, in sports and other activities and entertainments.

**'A' list:** the most sought-after and popular Hollywood actors, cast by film producers with the aim of securing a large audience and the film's commercial success.
■ Actors who are not on the 'A' list sometimes have difficulty in finding work.

**al-Jazeera:** Arab satellite television station based in and subsidised by the Arab state of Qatar and widely viewed across the Arab world, launched in 1996.
■ Al-Jazeera's coverage of world events reflects Arab/Islamic perspectives and sensibilities. For many Muslims, it represents an alternative ideological standpoint from the dominant Western views presented by BBC World, Fox News and **Cable News Network** channels. Al-Jazeera also runs an expanding website and worldwide news service.

**alternative:** describes any media product that challenges **dominant** or **mainstream** values and ideology.
■ *e.g.* alternative comedy

**alternative comedy:** a form of comedy, often experimental, that challenges mainstream values and expectations, first developed in radio programmes such as the *Goon Show* (1950s) and then on television.
■ Alternative comedy often shocks the audience by extreme, unexpected or unorthodox representations, e.g. in *The League of Gentlemen* one of the comic themes is cannibalism.
■ *e.g.* *Monty Python's Flying Circus* (1970s), *Not the 9 O'clock News* (1970s/1980s), *The Young Ones* (1980s), *Who Dares Wins* (1980s), *The Fast Show* (1990s), *The League of Gentlemen* (2000) and *Little Britain* (2004)

**Althusser, Louis (1918–90):** French **Marxist** sociologist with a particular interest in the role of the media in supporting **dominant ideology** and in the symbolic order separating us from reality.
■ He saw the media as an **ideological state apparatus** operating entirely in the interest of the state and the ruling **elite**.
■ He devised the term **interpellation** to describe the way an individual is identified and addressed as a subject by the media and at the same time made to respond to the media's cues.

**ambient media:** advertising media found in everyday objects rather than the traditional advertising media of press, radio, television and films.
■ *e.g.* computer mouse mats, litter bins, football goal nets, restaurant serviettes, beer mats, Formula One racing cars

**ambient sound:** the natural sound present in any location.

■ This could be birds singing, running water, the sound of the sea or traffic noise. When this sound is incorporated in a film narrative in such a way that it is audible to the characters, it becomes diegetic, i.e. part of the story.

**ambulance chasing:** a derogatory term used to describe the journalistic practice of pursuing stories involving death or injury in order to profit from them in terms of journalistic copy and photographs and to satisfy the voyeuristic curiosity of an audience.

■ The term is also applied to lawyers and attorneys who seek to profit from human suffering.

■ *e.g.* Controversy was caused when photographers sought to profit from the sale of images of the car crash in which Princess Diana died in 1997. In this case, no British newspapers would publish the photographs.

**American Dream:** a cultural myth based on the belief that the USA is a land of promise and opportunity where anyone who works hard can achieve all the good things in life, notably love, esteem and wealth.

■ The origins of the myth lie with the American Declaration of Independence, which emphasises the equality of all humanity and the right to 'life, liberty and the pursuit of happiness'. At the time this document was written many wealthy American colonial citizens were slave owners.

■ Belief in the American Dream can lead to a conflict between the desire for wealth and material happiness and the means by which this ideal is achieved. In many gangster movies, the ends are seen to justify the means and the protagonist can become an anti-hero in the eyes of the audience.

■ The realities of US society are far from those of the idealised version and are sometimes called the American nightmare.

■ e.g. *Rocky* (John G. Avildsen, 1976), in which Sylvester Stallone boxes his way from rags to riches; in both *Erin Brockovich* (Steven Soderbergh, 2000) and *Pretty Woman* (Garry Marshall, 1990) Julia Roberts plays characters who overcome poor backgrounds and adversity in order to climb the social ladder.

■ *TIP* The myth of the American Dream is important because it forms the background ideology of media products from across all genres but in particular of film and television productions.

**American nightmare:** phrase used by Black Power politician Malcolm X (1925–65) to express his sense of the inequalities, particularly with regard to the link between race and opportunity, experienced by black Americans.

■ The phrase is now used to refer to the contradictions and conflicts found in all those areas of US society where different ethnic and religious groups face discrimination and where extremes of poverty and wealth are common.

■ Gun crime levels are so high that many Americans keep and use guns for self-protection.

■ Community values conflict with a culture of individualism and the pursuit of material goals.

■ Corporate power is so great as to control many aspects of US life.

■ Fears of all kinds, particularly of terrorism since 9/11, have created a defensive collective mentality, reflected in media texts.

■ *TIP* All these aspects of US society can be evident in the representations, values and ideologies of films and television productions, e.g. *Bowling for Columbine* (Michael Moore, 2002), *Donnie Darko* (Richard Kelly, 2001), *American History X* (Tony Kaye, 1998), *The Virgin Suicides* (Sophia Coppola, 1999), *Panic Room* (David Fincher, 2002) and *The Pledge* (Sean Penn, 2001).

**analogue:** in media technology, a method of recording visual and sound images. Analogue technology represents the shape or appearance of an object in an unbroken form.

■ Traditional film is analogue as it runs through the camera recording images in an unbroken sequence.

■ Radio waves as a continuous form carrying sound signals are analogue, as opposed to digital computerised technology, which breaks up a signal into digital units.

■ *TIP* Analogue technology is now being replaced by digital systems.

**anchor (also known as 'anchorage'):** in semiology, any caption or key element that fixes the meaning of an image and directs the viewer toward a preferred reading.

■ *e.g.* Newspapers use captions to anchor the meaning of photographs.

**anchor man/woman:** the key presenter of a news or current affairs transmission who provides continuity links and creates an identity for the programme.

■ *e.g.* Jon Snow *Channel 4 News*, David Dimbleby BBC1 *Question Time*

**angle:** the point of view adopted by a journalist in relation to a story.

■ *e.g.* When reporting an earthquake, emphasis may be given to the number of dead and injured, the speed of international reaction, the response of the local authorities, the build quality of collapsed buildings, the miraculous rescue of a baby, the hope of finding more survivors, the economic consequences for the region, the effort to raise money internationally etc.

**anime:** Japanese term for a type of animated cartoon ranging from the silly to the sexy and serious.

■ Japanese animation products are directed at all age groups and (together with manga comics, their print form) have become increasingly influential in Western media products.

**a**

■ Anime is characterised by heavily stylised backgrounds and fantasy or science-fiction themes. Motion is simulated with moving backgrounds and static characters who often have exaggerated facial expressions with large heads and childlike eyes.

■ *e.g.* *Spirited Away* (Hayao Miyazaki, 2003)

■ *TIP* *Kill Bill: Vol. 1* (Quentin Tarantino, 2003) was influenced by Japanese anime productions.

**antagonist:** the principal opposing figure or villain in a narrative, set in binary opposition against the protagonist.

**anthropomorphism:** the attribution to animals or inanimate objects of human feelings, emotions and other characteristics.

■ Disney cartoons have always used anthropomorphism to engage audiences with the experiences of animal characters, e.g. *Bambi* (David Hand, 1942).

**anti-climax:** a point in a narrative, following the climax or emotional high point, which lets down or deflates the experience, leaving the reader/viewer with a sense of disappointment.

■ *e.g.* In films about the sinking of the Titanic, there is often an anti-climax once the ship has sunk. In the most recent version, *Titanic* (James Cameron, 1997), the problem is solved by the tension created around the death of Jack (Leonardo Di Caprio) in the freezing water and the subsequent rapid image sequence of the life of Rose (Kate Winslet), ending with her death and dreamlike return to the sunken ship and its ghosts.

**anti-hero:** the protagonist in a narrative who lacks the qualities of an archetypal hero but nevertheless attracts the sympathy and support of the audience or reader.

■ *e.g.* Jim in *Rebel without a Cause* (Nicholas Ray, 1955), played by James Dean

**anti-narrative:** a text that challenges the traditional idea of sequential linear narrative by using flashbacks, unrelated images and altered time sequences.

■ *TIP* French director François Truffaut famously remarked that all film texts must have 'a beginning, middle and an end' to which fellow director Jean-Luc Godard replied: 'Yes, but not necessarily in that order.'

**AOL Time Warner:** see Time Warner.

**AP:** see Associated Press.

**aperture:** the opening of a camera lens which can be adjusted to control the amount of light entering a camera and the exposure of the film.

**archetype:** an often-repeated character type or representation which is instantly recognisable to an audience.

■ Like **stereotypes**, archetypes are a form of character shorthand, enabling film makers to establish character identity instantly and to rely on an audience's prior knowledge.

■ *e.g.* the seductive *femme fatale* in *film noir*, the smart-suited Italianate gangster in **gangster** genre, the whiskered 'old timer' in a 1940s' **Western** (famously played by George 'gabby' Hayes)

**arc shot:** a type of camera shot in which the camera circles the subject, often creating a disorientating effect.

**artefact:** a term sometimes used in media industries to describe a media product.

**art house:** a cinematic production generated by aesthetic and cultural production values rather than commercial considerations.

■ Art house productions are not usually designed to attract mass audiences since they do not follow formulaic genre and narrative structures, nor do they have big budgets or the backing of large media organisations. As a result, they are not carried by major film **distributors.**

**artwork:** the pictorial element of a print-based advertisement as opposed to the written **copy.**

**ASA:** see Advertising Standards Authority.

**aspect ratio:** the height to width ratio of a television or cinema screen.

■ Differences in aspect ratio can be a problem where widescreen films are shown unadjusted on standard televisions and the top and bottom of the picture is lost. Even with adjustments, elements of the original production can be distorted.

**aspirational media:** advertising term applied to magazines whose readership aspires to the lifestyle represented in the magazine's contents and its advertising, while not having the immediate financial means to achieve it.

■ Advertisers increasingly recognise that spending and consumption patterns are determined by aspirations rather than by current demographic status. People will buy ahead of their status, aspiring to an ideal image of themselves constructed by advertising and media **representations.**

■ *e.g.* Readers of *House and Garden* magazine may aspire to a luxury apartment or country house, readers of motoring magazines may aspire to own an advertised sports car, readers of *Vogue* may aspire to own the clothes featured.

**Associated Newspapers:** newspaper publishing company, a subsidiary of the *Daily Mail* and General Trust Ltd, established in 1905 by Alfred Harmsworth (later Lord Northcliffe).

■ It publishes the *Daily Mail*, the *Mail on Sunday*, the *Evening Standard* (London region), *Loot, Metro* (**freesheet** newspapers) and a large number of regional titles.

- Associated Newspapers is the only major British newspaper publisher still in the hands of the original founding family (Harmsworth/Rothermere).

**Associated Press (AP):** the largest and oldest global news agency, founded in 1848.
- It has 3,700 employees, 240 bureaus, an online news service, a television news service and a 24-hour radio service.

**Associated Television (ATV):** one of the original, regional Independent Television franchise companies, covering the London area.
- The first chairman, Lew Grade (later Lord Grade), famously described the contract as 'a licence to print money'.

**attitudes, beliefs and values:** terms commonly used when discussing the audience for media products and the factors influencing the reception of media messages.
- Attitudes are the positions people adopt in relation to a particular issue, e.g. being for or against foxhunting.
- Beliefs are deeply held views, e.g. a belief in the principle of human equality or a belief in God.
- Values represent the moral or ideological structure within which beliefs and attitudes are formed, e.g. belief in Christianity or Islam.
- All these factors affect the reception of media texts. Research also focuses on the ways in which media content influences the formation, representation and reproduction of attitudes, beliefs and values.

**ATV:** see Associated Television.

**audience:** *key concept* the groups or individuals targeted by producers as the intended consumers of media texts. Owing to the wide availability of media texts, the actual viewers, readers or listeners may not be those originally targeted.
- Audience studies are usually structured in terms of gender, age and social and cultural background, and are concerned with the circumstances in which media texts, are consumed and the nature and the consequences of this consumption.
- The identification of an audience is a vital ingredient for the successful production and marketing of a media text.
- Considerations of audience motivation and behaviour are a key focus of attention in both active and passive audience theories.

**audience flow:** in television scheduling, the extension of an audience by, for example, placing a new comedy after an established one, or by clustering similar programmes together.
- *e.g.* In BBC 2's *History Zone* several related programmes are run sequentially.

**audience participation:** the practice of involving the audience in television and radio productions by inviting their votes or opinions or their direct participation in the activities that form the basis of the programme.
■ Developments in interactive technology allow viewers to vote directly and to see their votes influence events on screen, e.g. *Pop Idol, The X Factor, Fame Academy* and *I'm a Celebrity…Get Me out of Here.*

**audience profile:** an advertising and marketing term for the demographic and personal characteristics of members of the target audience for a media product.
■ Profiling and targeting a specific audience is increasingly important in the world of lifestyle marketing and niche marketing and audience fragmentation.
■ Audience profiles include some or all of the following: age, gender ethnicity, employment status, social status, marital status, attitudes, beliefs, and values, aspirations and patterns of consumption.

**audience studies:** see reception theory.

**audience theory:** any of various theories about the behaviour of audiences with regard to media texts.
■ Audience theories can be broadly divided into active models where the audience is seen as reacting to texts in a challenging, engaged way and passive models where the audience is seen as being influenced and manipulated directly by media content.
■ *e.g.* hypodermic theory, cultivation theory, effects theory, opinion leadership, reception theory, two-step flow, uses and gratifications theory

**Audit Bureau of Circulation (ABC):** an independent body, launched in 1931, in response to advertiser demand for independent verification of the claims made by the sales teams of newspapers and magazines, especially the national press then collectively known as Fleet Street.
■ *TIP* The ABC website is the most reliable source for the latest available circulation figures for all publications.

**auteurism:** a term coined in the French film journal *Cahiers du Cinéma* to describe the decisive, creative input of a film director in determining the stylistic and ideological treatment of a film.
■ An auteur is a master of film craft whose works have a distinctive personal signature, e.g. Stanley Kubrick.

**author:** individual responsible for the creation of a text.

**avant-garde:** an experimental style of film or television production that breaks new ground in taste, content and treatment, often attracting criticism from the mainstream for its radical challenge to the orthodox.

■ *e.g.* David Lynch's 1991 television production *Twin Peaks* introduced surrealist elements, including sound effects, camera and lighting techniques which disorientated viewers expecting a traditional soap opera treatment.

**Avid:** computer software video-editing package produced by the US company Avid Technology, the leading company in the non-linear digital editing and professional music industries.

■ Avid is seen as the industry standard product. Its flagship software program Media Composer was introduced in 1989 and allowed desktop editing of television and film productions.

■ The products, which include Film Composer, Symphony, and Avid Xpress, are used by music and film studios, postproduction facilities, radio broadcasters and television stations across the world, including the BBC, CNN and France Television. Avid also makes animation design software.

**back projection:** a filming technique in which live studio action is filmed in front of a screen displaying previously filmed material as background.

■ The technique was mostly used from the 1930s until the 1970s to provide outdoor locations and exotic backgrounds as settings for studio action.

■ Its most common use was for car journeys. The actors would sit in the front seat of a car facing the camera and pretend to drive, while the street they were driving down was projected behind them. The technique did not produce a realistic simulation of the driving experience but it was the easiest and cheapest way to portray actors in a moving car while recording sound.

■ *TIP* The technique can have unintentionally amusing effects, for example when the actions of the driver steering the car do not match the bends and turns in the road on the screen behind.

**BAFTA:** see British Academy of Film and Television Arts.

**balance:** in media output, where equal or proportionate time is given to various perspectives and points of view.

■ Balance is most important as a requirement of a public service remit, particularly in relation to political debate and elections covered by radio and television and, in the case of commercial broadcasters, monitored by Ofcom.

■ Newspapers have no obligation to seek balance but may still be reported to the Press Complaints Commission by aggrieved members of the public.

**banner (1):** an advertisement that is larger in width than in height, for example poster sites and some internet advertisements.

**banner (2):** a newspaper headline in large type that runs the width of the front page.

**BARB:** see Broadcasters' Audience Research Board.

**Barthes, Roland (1915–80):** French academic responsible for applying and extending Saussure's work on semiology to contemporary culture.

■ In his work *Mythologies* (1957), Barthes explores the language of **signs**, their combination from **paradigm** choices into **syntagms** of meaning and the concepts of **denotation**, **connotation** and **myth** as applied to film, advertising and the consumer objects that surround us.

■ Barthes also explores the structure of **narrative**, identifying five different **codes** by which a narrative engages the attention of an audience, most importantly the **enigma code** and the **action code**, but also the semic, symbolic and cultural codes.

**Baudrillard, Jean (1929–):** French **postmodernist** sociologist who argues that reality has been replaced by simulated worlds, or **simulacra**, composed of images and events ranging from Disneyland to the television news.

■ *TIP* Critics argue that Baudrillard is too concerned with the **subjective** and that his work is lacking in empirically based or evaluative studies of actual media content and representations.

**BBC:** see British Broadcasting Corporation.

**BBFC:** see British Board of Film Classification.

**BCC:** see Broadcasting Complaints Commission.

**BCU (short for 'big close up'):** a close-up camera shot, particularly of an actor's face, showing prominent detail and facial expression as a means of creating intimacy and audience engagement with the thoughts and emotions of the character.

***Benn's Media:*** comprehensive guide to all media businesses operating in the UK.

■ *TIP* *Benn's Media* is available at larger libraries and has an internet site. It is a valuable resource when researching media companies, their ownership and range of activities.

**Berliner (also known as 'midi'):** a newspaper size between a **tabloid** and **broadsheet**, popular in Europe.

■ It uses a slightly larger format than that of the tabloid, usually about 470 mm by 315 mm.

■ The format is used by many continental European newspapers, including quality dailies such as *Le Monde* in France and *La Republica* in Italy.

**BFI:** see British Film Institute.

**bias:** the ideological slanting of a media text, usually factual reporting, to represent one point of view more favourably than another.

■ *e.g.* A party political broadcast is biased in favour of the party it represents.

■ *TIP* The word 'bias' is a noun. A piece of work showing evidence of bias is 'biased' (adjective).

**bibliography:** the section at the end of a media project that lists all the information sources.

■ A bibliography should be presented systematically using the Harvard system (author, date, title, and publisher). A filmography or list of films researched should include the film's title, the director and date of release. Television references should include the producer, title, series, broadcast channel and date of transmission. Internet references should include the address of the file (uniform resource locator).

■ *TIP* Remember that the person reading the bibliography may wish to look up the references cited and that ease of access, completeness and clarity are important if a good impression of the work is to be conveyed.

**big close up:** see BCU.

**big ten:** the ten major Hollywood film studios: Twentieth Century Fox, Metro-Goldwyn-Mayer (MGM), DreamWorks, Miramax, Sony Pictures, Paramount, Universal Studios, New Line Cinema, Walt Disney Pictures and Warner Brothers.

■ Disney owns Walt Disney Pictures and Miramax, Sony owns Sony Pictures and MGM, Time Warner owns New Line Cinema and Warner Brothers, and Vivendi owns Universal. This means that six giant corporations control the bulk of the film production and distribution industry.

**billboard advertisement:** large public-display advertisement posted on to a hoarding.

■ Billboard advertisements are a fairly crude way to reach an undefined mass audience and are often used to reinforce magazine and television advertisements by using the same images.

■ *TIP* Their indiscriminate and public nature can cause problems. When an exotic but highly retouched image of model Sophie Dahl naked appeared in an Opium perfume ad in women's magazines, there was no reaction as the purpose and intended audience were clear. When the same image appeared on billboards, there were complaints from mothers with small children who claimed it was indecent and others claiming the image distracted passing car drivers. The posters were withdrawn.

**binary opposition:** a term used by Claude Levi-Strauss as part of his argument that narratives are structured around oppositional elements in human culture, for example, good and evil, life and death, night and day, raw and cooked.

■ In contemporary media narratives, cowboys/Indians, black hats/white hats and gangsters/police represent binary oppositional forces. The audience is attracted by the dynamics of this conflict with the possible variations leading usually to the ultimate triumph of good.

**b**

■ Audiences are positioned in narratives to take sides and rewarded by the success of the side they are identified with. In *Black Hawk Down* (Ridley Scott, 2001), the audience is positioned alongside 'good' US forces in conflict with the 'bad' native forces of Somali rebel leaders  In *Independence Day* (Roland Emmerich, 1996) the world — led by the US president — takes on and defeats an alien invasion.

■ *TIP* Binary narratives are also present in non-fiction texts, such as news reports and newspaper articles, where audiences are positioned on one side of an argument, e.g. security forces/terrorists, the police/criminals, management/unions.

**biopic:** a film based on the life story or biography of a real person.

■ *e.g.* *Ray* (Taylor Hackford, 2004) starring Jamie Foxx as Ray Charles

**bitmap:** method by which a computer stores and reproduces graphic images.

■ A bitmap consists of rows and columns of dots of a graphic image stored in a computer memory. It is the density of these dots, known as **resolution**, that determines how sharply an image is represented. The bitmap is translated into pixels for a display screen and monitor and into dots for a printer.

**black comedy:** a film or television production dealing with serious or disturbing subjects in a comic way.

■ Subjects might include war, personal injury, murder, crime, gangsterism, violence, suffering or serious social issues such as drug abuse.

■ *e. g.* Classic examples are *Dr Strangelove; or How I Learned to Stop Worrying and Love the Bomb* (Stanley Kubrick, 1964), a black comedy on the threat of nuclear war, and *A Clockwork Orange* (Stanley Kubrick, 1971), a black comedy on gang ultra violence, drug abuse, rape and state violence against the individual. More recent examples include *Trainspotting* (Danny Boyle, 1995), a black comedy on heroin abuse, and *Lock, Stock and Two Smoking Barrels* (Guy Ritchie, 1998) and *Snatch* (Guy Ritchie, 2000), both black-comedy treatments of organised crime, violence and murder.

**black feminism:** a feminist perspective which argues that black women's experience of inequality is more intense that white women's because it involves discrimination on racial and cultural grounds as well as gender grounds.

**blaxploitation film:** film of the 1960s and 1970s in which black actors featured in principal roles usually associated with whites.

■ The films were original in being directed primarily at black audiences and, although seen as exploitative, were in fact part of a changing attitude toward black characters and the representation of black culture.

■ *e.g.* *Shaft* (Gordon Parks, 1971)

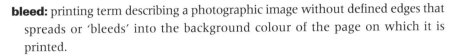

**bleed:** printing term describing a photographic image without defined edges that spreads or 'bleeds' into the background colour of the page on which it is printed.

**blockbuster:** a big-budget Hollywood film.
■ Blockbusters combine known stars and celebrities with fast-moving action narratives, spectacular sets and many special effects. Heavily marketed and promoted, they are designed to generate maximum box-office takings to justify the large sums invested. The emphasis is on hype and spectacle rather than on plot and character development.
■ Blockbusters are part of an extensive **merchandising** operation designed to sell associated products. Ideologically, they are dominated by US cultural perspectives and values.
■ *e.g.* *Spider-Man* (Sam Raimi, 2002)

**blue screen:** a process in special effects work whereby action is filmed in front of a blue screen which is then removed from the film footage and replaced by different images.
■ *e.g.* The science fiction film *Contact* (Robert Zemeckis, 1997) involved extensive use of blue screen to place actor Jody Foster in deep space and exotic locations.
■ *TIP* The technique demands a great deal from actors who have to imagine the setting they are being placed in while they are in reality standing in front of a blue screen in a studio.

**B-movie:** a supporting film in traditional cinema showings of the 1930s to 1960s.
■ B-movies were low budget and filmed on black and white stock. Although many were unmemorable, B-movies did provide openings for experimental forms and unknown actors and directors.
■ B-movies allowed cinemas to offer a value-for-money 'double bill' that appealed to audiences.

**Bobo doll experiment:** an experiment on social learning and the transmission of aggression carried out by Albert Bandura in 1961.
■ Bandura got children to watch a video where an actor aggressively attacked a plastic clown called a Bobo doll, hitting and punching it and throwing it around. The children were taken to a room where there were attractive toys they were not allowed to touch. They were then taken to another room with dolls similar to the ones seen in the video. Bandura observed that 88% of the children then imitated the aggressive behaviour they had seen. Eight months later 40% of the children still reproduced the same violent behaviour.
■ Bandura concluded that children learn aggressive responses through imitating others and also indirectly from the media, and that consequently aggressive behaviour could be modified if identified early.

■ The work is often used to justify the view that media violence encourages violence in television and film viewers, particularly where impressionable children are still learning appropriate social responses.

■ There is no evidence in Bandura's work that aggressive behaviour toward a doll would be transferred to a person.

■ *TIP* Great care should be taken not to claim that Bandura's research 'proves' media violence affects behaviour. It merely demonstrates that children who have watched a video of adults attacking a plastic doll might be encouraged to do the same.

**body double:** an actor whose body is used to replace that of another actor for particular scenes.

■ Body doubles may be used for dangerous shots, where stunt actors are employed, for those involving sexual contact or nudity or for shots where the actor's body may not be considered suitable.

■ *e.g.* In *Pretty Woman* (Garry Marshall, 1990), Julia Roberts used a body double for nude shots and even on the poster advertising the film. Gwyneth Paltrow in *Shallow Hal* (Farrelly Brothers, 2001) was replaced by a body double to portray a much heavier character. Brad Pitt used a double for his legs in *Troy* (Wolfgang Peterson, 2004) as they were considered too skinny for the role of the Greek hero Achilles.

**Bollywood:** term for the Indian film industry, based in Bombay (Mumbai).

■ The industry produces a large number of films, based on traditional Indian themes involving exotic sets and dance routines, complicated romances between female dancers/singers and idealised male hero figures, who are often based on characters from Hindu religion, myth and folk tale.

■ Indian films are aimed specifically at an Indian audience but in recent years their influence has been felt more widely, e.g. *Monsoon Wedding* (Mira Nair, 2002), with themes bridging Western and Indian culture, was an international success.

■ *e.g.* Traditional Bollywood musical classics include: *Sahib Bibi aur Ghulum* (Guru Dutt, 1962), *Bandini* (Blimal Roy, 1963), *Coolie* (Manmohan Desai, 1983).

**bootleg:** illegal copy of a media product, such as an audio tape, CD or film.

■ Bootlegs of movies are often produced by simply pointing a video camera at the screen during a showing. They are often of low quality but are used to break release deadlines and provide early, cheap and readily available copies of texts which are either restricted or in limited supply.

***Brad* (short for 'British Rates and Data'):** the standard comprehensive directory of advertising opportunities, providing information on where adverts can be placed and how much they will cost.

■ *Brad* provides essential information for those buying and selling advertising. It is printed monthly and is also available online. It has 13,500 entries covering all media from newspapers to hot air balloons, litter bins, bus shelters and cinema posters. It lists 1,500 advertising agencies and 3,000 advertisers, with contact details, audience and readership figures, advertising rates and, where appropriate, production data.

■ *Brad* is used by advertising agencies to plan advertising schedules, and helps media owners sell advertising space and gain more advertising.

**brand:** an important advertising concept whereby a product is given an identity and associated characteristics that appeal to consumers.

■ Once established in one product area, brand identity can be transferred to other products carrying with it all the related associations. Celebrities can be constructed as brands and used to advertise a range of products.

■ *e.g.* David Beckham as a brand can advertise trainers and razors and mobile phones, bringing together unrelated products through his lifestyle, ease of recognition, and personal popularity. Marlboro, with connotations of outdoor rugged masculinity, can cease being associated with cigarettes and transfer itself to fashionable clothing.

**bricolage:** French term for the random assembly by culture groups of various cultural signifiers to form new and often unintended meanings.

■ *e.g.* Skinheads combined shaved heads, Doc Martin work boots, Levi 501 jeans, Ben Sherman shirts and old fashioned bracers to create a new uniform that reflected their working-class values and group identity. Punks adopted fashion items from a variety of different sources, including bin liners and safety pins.

**bridging shot:** a camera shot that shows a passage of time or change of location as a means of connecting one scene to another.

■ *e.g.* Typical bridging shots of the passage of time include a shot of a tree showing all four seasons in quick succession to represent the passing of a year.

**brief:** the descriptive outline of a set task, usually designed for execution by a specific individual and providing clear guidelines on what has to be achieved.

■ *TIP* A brief is often prepared by one person to be completed by another but it can also be designed by the individual concerned. It should be detailed, easy to follow and include a title, a rationale or explanation of the task, the audience or recipient for the outcome, resources available, evaluation criteria and a time scale for completion.

**British Academy of Film and Television Arts (BAFTA):** the UK's leading organisation for promoting and rewarding productions judged to be the best in film, television and interactive media. BAFTA was founded in 1947 as the British Film Acadamy.

- The organisation is famous for its increasingly high-profile award ceremonies, covering film, television, and children's and interactive entertainment, which it has attempted to make the rival of the US Academy Awards.
- BAFTA Awards are now sponsored by the mobile phone company Orange.

**British Board of Film Censors:** a public body established in 1912 to standardise the censorship and classification of films (previously the role of local authorities) and to provide a national standard acceptable to all, renamed the British Board of Film Classification (BBFC) in 1985.

- Local authorities, however, reserved the right to censor or even ban films they felt were unsuitable viewing.
- The board changed its name in 1985 to reflect a less censorial and paternalistic approach to the viewing of the visual image, particularly with regard to consensual sex between adults.

**British Board of Film Classification (BBFC):** the organisation responsible for classifying and certificating films, DVDs and videos for public showing and — in the case of videos and DVDs — also for private viewing. The BBFC replaced the British Board of Film Censors in 1985 following the wider remit required under the Video Recordings Act of 1984, which included the classification of videos for home viewing.

- The BBFC sees its role as classification within acceptable guidelines rather than censorship. It has been involved in liberalising restrictions on visual material directed at adult audiences. It classifies films under the following categories:
  - Uc: suitable for pre-school children
  - U: suitable for audiences aged 4 and over
  - PG: suitable for any age but parental guidance should be given
  - 12A: no child under 12 may see the film unless accompanied by an adult
  - 12: suitable viewing for aged 12 and over
  - 15: suitable viewing for aged 15 and over
  - 18: adult viewing suitable for aged 18 and over
- Categorisation is based on the number and type of swear words, the amount of sex and violence or sexual violence or drug-taking any film contains, and the principle concern is the protection of children and young people from material deemed disturbing, harmful or corrupting. For example, certain four-letter words would be allowed only once in a film rated 12, any more instances and a 15 certificate would be given.
- Classification of videos and DVDs for home viewing can be more severe than for cinema release because of the private nature of the viewing environment.
- Category R18 (R means restricted) is reserved for sexually explicit material sold or shown only in licensed sex shops and cinemas.

b

- Ken Loach's film *Sweet Sixteen* (2002) was refused a 15 certificate (even though it was acted by and targeted at 15–16 year olds) because it contained a four-letter word still regarded by the board as unacceptable for an under-18 audience.
- *TIP* Film classification can be controversial. In 1998 the film *Crash* (David Cronenberg, 1996) was banned as indecent by the London Borough of Westminster even though it had been granted an 18 certificate by the board. Film goers had to cross over into the neighbouring borough of Camden to view the film. The BBFC website is an excellent source of information on censorship, film classification and other matters relating to media effects debates.

**British Broadcasting Corporation (BBC):** the principal public service broadcasting organisation in the UK.

- Founded as a company in 1922, it was remodelled as the BBC in 1927 when it was granted a charter and a 10-year renewable licence to broadcast by Parliament.
- The BBC had a monopoly position until Independent Television (ITV) was founded in 1955. Its remit was to inform, to instruct and to entertain the nation, while maintaining an aloof respectability as a defender of the establishment. Its role was challenged by the advent of ITV and again by deregulation in 1992.
- While retaining a public service role and the licence fee, the BBC has become a more commercially minded organisation in the last 10 years, openly competing in the market place and buying programmes from independent producers.
- The original BBC television channel was retitled BBC 1 with the launch of BBC 2 in 1962 following the Pilkington Committee's recommendation that the BBC should be granted a second channel. The committee's decision was seen as an endorsement of the quality output of the BBC and a criticism of ITV's populism. BBC 2 was to concentrate on the arts and minority programming, leaving BBC 1 to compete with the ITV network and its single channel.
- The BBC currently provides two digital channels: BBC 3, created from BBC Choice and aimed at a young mainstream market, and BBC 4, derived from BBC Knowledge with a schedule built around arts and culture programming.
- *TIP* The future of the licence fee (worth £2.4 billion a year after 2003) is a source of constant debate, with operators such as BSkyB claiming that it provides the BBC with an unfair commercial advantage.

**British Film Institute (BFI):** an organisation founded in 1933 to promote an understanding and appreciation of British film culture.

- Supported by royal charter, the institute is funded by the government via the Film Council and is responsible for supporting a wide range of activities. It runs the National Film Theatre and the London Imax cinema, has the largest film library in the world, sponsors film festivals, has an education division and publishes the magazine *Sight and Sound*.

**British New Wave:** a term borrowed from the French New Wave of the same era, used to describe a similarly social realist style of independent film, produced between 1959 and 1963 and associated with the work of Karel Reisz, Tony Richardson, John Schlesinger and Lindsay Anderson.

■ The films were shot on black and white stock, with bleak, northern, industrial, working-class locations and realistic representations of sexual relationships and working-class life. Lead characters were usually alienated working-class outsiders.

■ The movement was largely unsupported by the British film industry and some directors sought financial backing from outside the UK for later productions. The films' distinctive character was caught up in the wider social and cultural changes of the 1960s and 'Swinging London', e.g. *Morgan: A Suitable Case for Treatment* (Karel Reisz, 1966).

■ The films of Ken Loach provide the closest contemporary link to the movement, e.g. *Sweet Sixteen* (2002).

■ *e.g.* *Saturday Night and Sunday Morning* (Karel Reisz, 1960), *A Taste of Honey* (Tony Richardson, 1961), *The Loneliness of the Long Distance Runner* (Tony Richardson, 1962), *A Kind of Loving* (John Schlesinger, 1962), *This Sporting Life* (Lindsay Anderson, 1963)

**British Rates and Data:** see *Brad*.

**British Sky Broadcasting (BSkyB or Sky):** the company name of Rupert Murdoch's television satellite channel in the UK and Europe, part of the News Corporation.

**broadband:** a system of transmission where a single fibre-optic telecommunications cable, with a wide band of frequencies, carries multiple signals.

■ Broadband allows for a high-speed internet connection, with telephone services on the same line, replacing traditional analogue dial-up services.

■ Large video, audio and three-dimensional files can be downloaded. The speed of broadband is subject to varying definitions, with some sources starting at 56 kilobytes per second, but with British Telecom's definition standing at 500 bits per second.

■ Broadband allows for a return signal, allowing interactive services such as banking to operate.

**broadcast:** the wide and random dissemination of media messages (broadly cast, i.e. spread over a wide area).

■ A broadcast message is available to anyone who tunes in to the relevant radio or television transmission service.

**Broadcasters' Audience Research Board (BARB):** an organisation, owned by the BBC and the Independent Television Companies Association, whose task it is to measure audiences for television companies.

**Broadcasting Act of 1990:** an Act of Parliament intended as the first step on the road to deregulation of British broadcasting.

■ The 1990 Act replaced the Independent Broadcasting Authority with the Independent Television Commission, established the Radio Authority to monitor radio output and the Broadcasting Standards Council, and lifted some restrictions on media ownership. It also made provision for the establishment, by franchise, of Channel 5 (later renamed Five).

**Broadcasting Act of 1996:** an Act of Parliament that led to the 1998 merger of the Broadcasting Standards Council and the Broadcasting Complaints Commission, further relaxed restrictions on ownership, regulated some cross-media ownership and established a framework for the introduction of digital television, with a switch-off date for the analogue signal set for 2012.

**Broadcasting Complaints Commission (BCC):** a public body established in 1980 to monitor the contents of public broadcasting and respond to complaints made by members of the public, and merged with the Broadcasting Standards Council to form the Broadcasting Standards Commission in 1998.

■ As an independent statutory body, its task was to consider and adjudicate upon complaints about material broadcast, both programmes and advertisements.

**Broadcasting Standards Commission:** title of the merged (1998) Broadcasting Complaints Commission and Broadcasting Standards Council, replaced by Ofcom in 2003.

■ The commission monitored all licensed broadcasting services and responded to concern from members of the general public. Its remit covered sex, violence, stereotyping, language and the representation of disasters, religions, alcohol, drugs, and smoking.

**Broadcasting Standards Council (BSC):** a public body established by the Broadcasting Act of 1990 to monitor broadcasting standards, and merged with the Broadcasting Complaints Commission to form the Broadcasting Standards Commission in 1998.

**broadsheet:** full-size newsprint (approximately 400mm by 590mm when folded), the original standard size for a newspaper.

■ In Britain, the term has come to be associated with quality publications in contrast to tabloid newspapers. However, the impracticality of large newspapers led to the introduction of tabloid or compact versions of former broadsheet newspapers in the early 2000s.

- *The Times*, a former broadsheet newspaper, is now only available in tabloid form.
- The *Independent*, a pioneer of the change, is still available in both formats.

**browser:** a computer software package used to view, download, surf or interact with web pages on the internet.
- The most popular browsers are Internet Explorer, Netscape and Mosaic.

**BSC:** see Broadcasting Standards Council.

**BSkyB:** see British Sky Broadcasting.

**buddy movie:** a film that focuses on the relationship between two characters, traditionally male but more recently of either sex.
- Contemporary buddy films can include heterosexual, homosexual and ambiguous relationships.
- *e.g.* A classic example of a traditional buddy movie is *Butch Cassidy and the Sundance Kid* (George Roy Hill, 1969). A classic feminist variation is *Thelma and Louise* (Ridley Scott, 1991).

**Buena Vista Pictures:** a collection of film studios, all subsidiaries of the Disney company, including Miramax, Hollywood Pictures and Touchstone Pictures.

**burst:** a short, intense advertising campaign, usually focused on television and radio.

**Butler, Judith (1956–):** professor of comparative literature and rhetoric at the University of California, Berkeley. Butler is associated with 'queer theory' — studies that question sexuality, gender identity and their representation in the media.
- Butler argues that gender identity is a construction that can be changed, rather than a reflection of any fixed 'inner self'. Traditional views of masculinity and femininity are therefore social constructions and can be challenged and altered.

**by-line:** the use of a journalist's name on a newspaper article or report.
- Not all articles are attributed to a particular journalist and a by-line is recognition of an author's status.

**Cable News Network (CNN):** an international news organisation with worldwide satellite and internet coverage, owned by Time Warner, with headquarters in Atlanta, Georgia, USA.
- CNN's world news coverage is seen as an example of news values being globalised in line with dominant Western ideologies.

***Cahiers du Cinéma:*** a French film magazine, the centre of debates on the direction of cinema, in particular the need to reflect contemporary life and experience.
- Founded by André Bazin in 1951, it gave rise to the *Nouvelle Vague* (French New Wave) of directors.

**cameo:** a brief appearance by a famous actor in a film production.
- A cameo is often used to increase the marketing appeal of a film as the cameo actor's name can appear on posters and publicity materials. Cameo actors can often demand large fees for a brief appearance.
- *e.g.* Marlon Brando made a cameo appearance as Superman's father in *Superman* (Richard Donner, 1978).

**camp:** a comic performance where characteristics are exaggerated to the point of absurdity for comic effect.
- Camp representations of homosexuality were a common form in television situation comedy before greater acceptance of gay culture and more politically correct representations became the norm.
- *e.g.* *Are You Being Served?* (1970s)

**campaign:** an organised range of activities and texts, orchestrated and delivered by the mass media but designed and directed by groups seeking to persuade or influence public opinion and behaviour.
- *e.g.* a campaign to achieve the re-election of a politician; an advertising campaign to achieve increased sales of a product

**Cannes Film Festival:** the most prestigious of the European film festivals, based in Cannes in the south of France.

■ Begun in 1946, Cannes shows new films, awarding the coveted Palme d'Or prize to the best.

■ Other European film festivals include those of Berlin and Venice.

**canted shot:** see Dutch angle.

**capitalism:** an economic system in which the production and distribution of goods and services in society is organised via a free market for the purpose of maximising profits.

■ Under capitalism, an elite ruling class of property and wealth owners hires labour in exchange for wages and uses the political system to resist any social and economic change that would challenge their hegemony.

■ Supporters of capitalism argue that a free market is the most effective way of producing goods and services in response to consumer demand, with the pressure of market forces encouraging efficient operation in the face of competition.

■ The most comprehensive critique of capitalism is provided by Marxism, which sees capitalism as the economic exploitation of one class by another. Capitalist power is sustained by agencies like the media, which help to maintain a false consciousness among the masses, who are therefore unaware of their exploitation. Marxism predicts that class conflict leading to revolution will eventually cause the collapse of the capitalist system.

**caption:** a brief, written text designed to anchor and stabilise the meaning of a pictorial text.

**Carlton:** former UK broadcasting and media company which held a major stake in commercial television in London and the Midlands until it merged with Granada in 2003 to form a single commercial television company, ITV plc.

■ The Carlton/Granada merger caused some concern for the future of Independent Television News as principal UK news supplier, as its contract to supply news could be subject to competitive tender (in 2005, Sky News has already won the contract to supply Five News), and for regional broadcasting in general, since both the merging companies had traditions of regional identity which some feared would be lost.

**cartoon:** a short animated feature film.

■ Cartoons were originally based on photographs of a succession of drawings but are now largely produced using digital technology.

■ *e.g.* Famous companies associated with cartoon production include Warner Brothers (Time Warner): *Loony Tunes* with Daffy Duck and Bugs Bunny (1940s).

**C**

**case study:** an in-depth study of a person, event or social phenomenon, involving the collection, analysis and evaluation of data which can then be used to suggest links with wider issues.
- Case studies are in the empirical research tradition. They are important in such areas as research into the exposure of children to sex and violence on television.
- *e.g.* Bandura's 1961 Bobo doll experiment

**cathode-ray tube (CRT):** a display and electron gun used in traditional television sets and traditional computer monitors.
- The CRT screen is lined with a phosphorous material, arranged as millions of tiny pixels, which glow when struck by a stream of electrons. At the back of the monitor, a set of electron guns produces the stream of electrons, starting from the top, scanning rapidly from left to right, then repeating the process so that the entire screen is drawn in a fraction of a second.
- CRTs are being challenged by new plasma screen technology, which allows for a flatter screen and a much-improved image.

**celebrity:** an individual who has become the focus of media attention and is therefore widely known and recognised by the public.
- Celebrities may or may not be associated with a particular career, lifestyle or activity. Increasingly, they can be ordinary individuals who become famous, and often wealthy, as a result of their lives and personalities being publicised by the media.
- The media can also create celebrities out of ordinary people by making them the focus of reality-television programmes such as *Big Brother*.

**censorship:** the practice, exercised by elite groups in authority, of monitoring and controlling media content by removing, suppressing or classifying elements deemed offensive or subversive for moral, political, economic, social or religious reasons.
- Relaxation of censorship has been a feature of Western-style pluralist democracies in recent years, although the protection of children is still cited as justification for the classification of films, videos and digital versatile (video) disks into categories restricted by age group (see British Board of Film Classification).
- Systems devised to restrict access to the internet and to television channels are available to protect children from sexually explicit, horrific or violent images.
- Censorship is still practised in fundamentalist or politically oppressive societies. The Taliban, when in power in Afghanistan, forbade the playing of music tapes and destroyed all that they found.

**Centre for Contemporary Cultural Studies:** department of Birmingham University devoted to the study of popular culture and the media.

- Under the direction of Stuart Hall in the 1970s and 1980s, the centre researched cultural issues from a Marxist perspective, for example, the representation of minority groups and races, the generation of moral panic and the resistance offered by subcultures to hegemonic ideology.
- The centre was also involved in the development of reception theory and the identification of dominant, negotiated and oppositional readings of media texts.

**CGI:** see computer-generated imagery.

**channel:** the means by which a media communication is effected, particularly in the context of television.

**Channel 4:** independent commercial television channel established in 1982 under the Independent Broadcasting Authority, with a brief to cover minority interests, the arts, documentary and film and to act as a complementary channel to Independent Television and the two British Broadcasting Corporation channels then current.

- Channel 4 developed a reputation for cutting-edge and challenging programming, often drawing criticism from television watchdog groups such as Mediawatch.
- Its support of the British Film Industry through its Film 4 division has been an important source of finance for independent producers, in spite of some financial failures and the need to reduce the status of the film division to a film channel.
- The high-status social profile of its audience has made the channel a favourite with advertisers and has helped secure its financial viability.

**Channel 5:** see Five.

**cheque book journalism:** the payment of large sums of money for sensational or topical first-hand accounts or exclusive photographs.

- Criminals, victims, celebrities and eye witnesses of spectacular or sensational events are the most likely beneficiaries (see kiss and tell, Press Complaints Commission).
- *e.g.* Victoria and David Beckham's nanny, Abbie Gibson, sold stories about their marital discord to the *News of the World* before being restrained by a court order.

**chiaroscuro lighting:** sharply contrasting lighting where strong highlights and dark shadows are used for dramatic and atmospheric effect.

- The term derives from the Italian 'chiaro', meaning 'clear' or 'bright', and 'oscuro', meaning 'dark'

**chick flick:** a film targeted at a young female audience.

■ Chick flicks are usually light, entertaining romances with contemporary music scores and comic undertones. Their narratives are directed at **mainstream** audiences and usually focus on the life experiences of their female protagonists.

■ *e.g.* *Legally Blonde* (Robert Luketic, 2001), *Legally Blonde 2* (Charles Herman-Wurmfeld, 2003), *Bridget Jones's Diary* (Sharon Maguire, 2001)

**Chomsky, Noam (1928–):** US academic, initially famous for his work in linguistics but more recently associated with a radical neo-Marxist critique of US society and the manipulative power of global media organisations.

■ Chomsky argues that news reporting is part of a process whereby the media seek to 'manufacture consent' in the interests of global **capitalism** and the 20% of the population he defines as the ruling **elite**. The bottom 80% of the population, with little real interest in world politics and economics, are manipulated and kept happy by a diet of popular media texts such as soap operas, celebrity gossip, sport and light entertainment.

■ He sees the relationship between profit-seeking media organisations and governments as one of mutual interest in supporting the **status quo** and **dominant ideology** and that this acts as a form of social control. Quotation: 'Any dictator would admire the conformity and obedience of the US media.'

■ *TIP* Chomsky's views are similar to those of the **Frankfurt School** and can be criticised for underestimating the resisting of **preferred readings** of media texts by increasingly cynical media audiences.

*cinéma vérité*: French term meaning 'truth cinema', used to describe a documentary technique that aims to reproduce real events as closely as possible.

■ The term is also applied to fictional narratives that aim to create a sense of truth through non-sophisticated techniques, raw edits and the use of hand-held cameras (see also **social realism, hand-held camera**).

**circular narrative:** a narrative in which the story-line ends where it began.

■ *e.g.* *Groundhog Day* (Harold Ramis, 1993), *Twelve Monkeys* (Terry Gilliam, 1995)

**circulation figures:** the audited numbers of newspapers sold over a given period.

■ Circulation figures are seen as a gauge of the health of a newspaper, particularly in the case of mass-circulation tabloids such as the **Sun**, with 3 million copies sold daily. Circulation is not the same as **readership**.

■ The 'quality' press operates on lower circulation, where figures ranging from 250,000 to just under 950,000 are acceptable.

■ *TIP* Overall circulation figures show a downward trend, particularly in the tabloid market. The website of the **Audit of Bureau of Circulation** is the most reliable source of circulation figures.

**cliff hanger:** a television or radio soap opera episode which ends with an unresolved dilemma or crisis in order to encourage the viewer or listener to tune in to the next episode.

**closed question:** a question to which the answer is restricted, assumed or obvious and which does not allow the person questioned a flexible response.

■ Questionnaires use closed questions to make the evaluation of results easier.

■ *e.g.* Do you enjoy or not enjoy watching soap operas? Do you like or dislike working with Adobe Premiere software? Do you prefer horror films or romantic comedies? Do you agree or disagree with film censorship?

**closed text:** a media text that is anchored in such a way as to restrict the number of ways in which it can be interpreted.

■ *e.g.* an image of diseased lungs with the caption 'Smoking Kills'

**closure:** the state of psychological harmony achieved when issues causing concern or distress to an individual are resolved and anxiety is removed or reduced.

■ In narrative, closure refers to the way in which polysemic stories are presented with certain preferred readings and satisfactory outcomes for the viewer or reader, which are usually in line with the values and expectations of dominant ideology.

■ *e.g.* In fairy-tales, 'they all lived happily ever after'; lessons are always to be learned when procedures for securing public safety fail; news programmes invariably end on a light-hearted and positive note.

**CNN:** see Cable News Network.

**code:** a system in which signs are organised.

■ Signifying codes consist of units that are organised in paradigms, from which one unit is chosen and then combined syntagmatically to create a text.

■ Codes convey meaning based on the agreed social and shared cultural experience of their users.

■ *e.g.* The cinematic codes of *film noir* (use of shadow lighting, Venetian blinds, gloomy settings, rain, guns, hats, trench coats, cigarette smoke) are instantly recognisable to film enthusiasts.

**cognition:** the mental process involved in perceiving, collecting and organising information about the world into a consistent and comprehensive framework of knowledge that reflects an individual's social and cultural environment.

■ In a media-saturated environment, much cognitive information is received via the media.

**cognitive dissonance:** the feeling of inconsistency and disharmony experienced by an individual when strongly held attitudes, beliefs and values are contradicted or challenged by new information or a new experience.

- The theory, developed by Leon Festinger (1919–89) in 1957, suggests that cognitive equilibrium or balance is a desired mental state and that individuals facing the experience of dissonance will adjust their attitudes and beliefs until a state of harmony is restored.
- It also suggests that, unless faced with overwhelming evidence, people will attempt to retain an existing viewpoint rather than adjust it in line with the new experience or information. This has implications for research into public-opinion formation and the influence of advertising and propaganda. It could also mean that once social and cultural **stereotypes** have formed in people's minds, they can be difficult to alter.
- *TIP* The theory implies that **campaigns** designed to change people's behaviour, for example, anti-smoking or healthy-eating campaigns, could face consumer resistance if they challenge deeply held views and past experience.

**colonialism:** the military, economic, political and cultural domination of African, South American, Australasian and Asian territories by occupying European powers from the sixteenth century through to the twentieth century.

- The system collapsed in the second half of the twentieth century as liberation movements secured the independence of most former colonies. However, the legacy of colonial occupation continues in the form of **cultural imperialism**, sustained by Western economic domination of global media industries.

**colour:** a signifying code from which paradigmatic elements can be selected to add to the meaning of a particular text.

- In Western culture, red can signify passion, danger or violence and its choice in a text can add this signification.
- Colour signification is subject to wide cultural variation, e.g. the colour of mourning in China is white, not black as in Western culture.

**coming-of-age film:** a film type that deals with puberty, adolescence, the growth of maturity and the search for sexual identity as set against the loss of innocence, childhood dreams and the difficulties of growing up.

- *e.g.* *Summer of 42* (Robert Mulligan, 1971), a rather sentimental, nostalgic example; *Sweet Sixteen* (Ken Loach, 2002), a hard-hitting, social realist text

**commercial radio:** radio broadcasts by licensed, privately owned stations begun in 1974 to counter the popularity of **pirate radio** stations.

- Commercial radio, originally served only local areas, but since deregulation in 1993 national stations such as Virgin Radio and Classic FM have been in operation.
- *TIP* Commercial stations have drawn audiences away from the **British Broadcasting Corporation**, whose share of national listening is expected to drop to around 30% by 2010.

**C**

**commercial television:** see Independent Television.

**commissioning editor:** the individual responsible for selecting and funding programmes and products made by independent production companies, usually employed by a film or television company.

■ With the increasing tendency of slimmed-down broadcasting organisations and corporates to outsource their programmes, this has become a key role in the deregulated industry.

■ The successful pitching of programme ideas to commissioning editors is a vital aspect of a production company's business.

**common sense:** term coined by Antonio Gramsci to describe the consensus in public opinion that forms around topics of social, political and economic concern in line with the ideology of the dominant class, as represented by the media.

■ One of the means by which power elites in society can maintain their position is by identifying their interests with common sense, thereby establishing the hegemony of dominant ideology as the right and natural way for society to be ordered. Common sense is difficult to challenge since it is assumed to indicate the obvious way to behave, a belief shared by all but deviants and subversives.

■ Mainstream media texts are seen as supporting dominant ideology and the common sense consensus.

**compact:** a differentiating term used by former broadsheet newspapers to describe their new tabloid format without attracting the negative connotations of that term.

■ Compact newspapers are generally popular with readers, although some do still prefer the larger broadsheet format.

■ Compacts are easier to read in crowded public places such as trains and are seen as more practical in the modern world.

**computer-generated imagery (CGI):** the application of computer software to generate a film image.

■ The first cinematic computer-generated images were used in *Terminator 2* (James Cameron, 1991) with the morphing of the robot T-1000.

■ CGI has allowed a return to the epic movie, with a 'cast of thousands' and enormous sets, including ancient cities, being generated by computers.

■ CGI productions have largely replaced traditional drawn animation products and are constantly developing ever more sophisticated technology, including live-action motion capture.

■ *e.g.* *Gladiator* (Ridley Scott, 2000), *Polar Express* (Robert Zemeckis, 2004)

**Condé Nast:** US publishing company, part of Advance Magazine Group and publishers of *House and Garden, Glamour,* **Vogue***, Vanity Fair* and *Tatler.*

**conglomerate:** an international company with a wide and varied range of commercial interests.

■ *e.g.* News Corporation, with its transcontinental interest in the publishing of books, magazines and newspapers, film and television production and satellite broadcasting, is a good example.

**connotation:** a meaning attributable to an image beyond the obvious **denotational** level.

■ Such meanings may be metaphorical, symbolic or culturally generated and will vary in line with the cultural background and **attitudes, beliefs and values** of the individual viewing the material.

■ *e.g.* An image of a red rose has connotations of New Labour, or England, or on a Valentine card can represent hot-blooded passion.

**consensus:** the middle ground of views and opinions within a society that is in line with **dominant ideology** and brokered by the media.

■ Consensus has always been an important aspect of social harmony, with groups agreeing to modify their attitudes and beliefs in order to generate social unity and solidarity. The increasing fragmentation of society, with its emphasis on individualism and the rights of minority groups, makes the concept of a middle-ground consensual framework more difficult to sustain.

**conspiracy theory:** a pessimistic and unrealistic view of the structure and operation of power within media organisations, which sees them as being controlled by a highly organised and coordinated elite.

■ The theory claims that there is an organised conspiracy by this elite to use media power to manipulate public opinion in line with their political views and economic interests. Chief conspirator in this paranoid model is usually Rupert Murdoch, although Italian prime minister and media tycoon Silvio Berlusconi is another good candidate.

■ Although there are elements of the theory present in **Frankfurt School** approaches and other **Marxist** critiques of media power, the belief in a coordinated conspiracy has little basis in fact.

■ *TIP* In the USA, conspiracy theory is associated with those disillusioned by the triumph of **right-wing** politics in their country and the past assassination of leading progressive politicians (e.g. Oliver Stone's 1991 film *JFK*, which argues that President Kennedy's 1963 assassination was part of a right-wing coup in the USA).

**construction:** the process behind the creation of all media texts.

■ All texts are the product of decisions relating to selection and are constrained and defined by the criteria used for that purpose, the choice available, and the order in which the elements are combined.

**C**

■ Constructions are based on choices made from **paradigmatic** codes, which are then formed into a **syntagmatic** ordered sequence to generate meaning (see **deconstruction**).

**consumerism:** the economic system and variation of **capitalism** based around the compulsive consumption of goods and services within a framework of **lifestyle marketing** and **advertising**.

■ Happiness, personal fulfilment and self-actualisation are presented as being achieved through the constant acquisition and accumulation of wealth and possessions.

■ Critics of consumerism point to the great inequalities of wealth and poverty existing in the world and the waste of valuable natural resources by a 'throw away' society. They argue that consumerism is sustained and developed by media and advertising industries' constructions and representations of an unobtainable ideal lifestyle, underpinned by an obsession with personal appearance and celebrity culture.

■ *e.g.* Television house-makeover programmes, such as *House Doctor* and *Hot Property*, generate dissatisfaction in their audiences and a desire to change the décor and contents of their homes. *House Doctor* is sponsored by the tile company Topps Tiles and *Hot Property* by the Abbey Building Society, both with an interest in selling and improving houses.

**content analysis:** a media research technique involving systematic analysis of the contents of a media product.

■ Content analysis is in the **empirical** tradition and involves testing observable evidence, for example, counting how often a particular element appears in any media product.

■ *e.g.* The representation of idealised female beauty in the photographs of fashion magazines such as *Vogue* can be assessed for ethnic and cultural variation. Results can then be used to argue for or against the **stereotyping** of a particular group.

**continuity editing:** an editing style that aims to present the text in a **linear** and chronological manner to emphasise the real-time movement of the **narrative** and to create a sense of realism for the viewer by giving the impression of continuous filming.

■ Continuity editing creates a narrative that approximates to the real experience of moving through time, even though screen time usually covers a much longer period. Audiences feel comfortable with a linear progression that reflects their everyday experience.

■ *TIP* The term 'continuity' also applies to the avoidance of errors in sequence or content, as when elements present in one scene are missing or altered in the next, e.g. *Gladiator* (Ridley Scott, 2000), in which Maximus the Gladiator turns his horse with his sword in his right hand in one scene and emerges from the turn with the sword in his left hand.

**convergence:** the coming together of new media technologies.

■ *e.g.* Television is now digital and interactive, with the potential for 1,000 channels and with technology available to download and store programmes; television can also be used for banking and shopping; internet webcams allow for visual interaction between users; music can be downloaded and burnt onto CDs and mobile phones can take and send pictures and access the internet.

**copy:** the written content of a newspaper or magazine as submitted to an editor for inclusion in a finished product.

**copy cat crimes:** crimes committed by individuals who appear to have imitated crimes either reported in the media or fictional crimes represented in film or television productions.

■ Supporters of **hypodermic theory** would argue that individuals are directly affected by what they hear and see in the media and that copy cat crimes are the result of exposure to media images. This can then become an argument for censorship (see **effects theory, censorship**).

**copyright:** the protection by law of the author and publisher of a media text from unauthorised reproduction of that text.

■ *TIP* The downloading of free music from the internet through such websites as Napster has created problems for the music industry and raised issues of copyright violation. Napster was forced to close in 2001 when record companies began a legal action for copyright infringement and the company was relaunched within the law in 2003, charging for music through a monthly subscription.

***Cosmopolitan (Cosmo):*** women's lifestyle magazine launched in 1972.

■ It was the first in a new generation of women's magazines to recognise the dramatic changes that had taken place in women's lives during the 1960s. It broke new ground under its original editor Helen Gurley Brown in advocating sexual and economic freedom for women, and in recognising that its readers were interested not only in men but also in appearance, mind, body and career.

■ The magazine was taken seriously by academics and supporters of the women's movement as an important contributor to the advancement of women's self-confidence, self-esteem and independence. It became a symbol of the changing times by discussing all aspects of sexuality openly for the first time, and it was the first mainstream women's magazine to publish naked male pin-ups.

■ In spite of its high profile on social and women's issues, *Cosmopolitan* is essentially a consumer-lifestyle magazine, published in 28 countries. Its high-spending readership makes it a magnet for advertisers — readers spend £1 billion a year on fashion goods and £1.4 billion on new cars.

■ *Cosmopolitan* is owned by National Magazines, which is part of the giant Hearst corporation and also publishes *Esquire, Good Housekeeping, She, Harpers Bazaar, Cosmo Girl,* and the US edition of *Marie Claire* (under licence from the French title-owner Hachette).

**counterculture:** a subculture that rejects the mainstream values of a society and offers a parallel, alternative way of life.

■ *e.g.* The Hippie counter culture of the 1960s challenged orthodox sexual morality, the work ethic and the family as core elements of mainstream society. Instead, Hippies advocated promiscuity (free love), dropping out (giving up work) and communal living, all sustained by rock music and the use of soft drugs. The *International Times* (*IT*) newspaper, *Oz Magazine* and comic books such as *Nasty Tales* represented the alternative values of the period. Punks, goths and grunge are all examples of youth countercultures.

**crab shot:** a type of shot which involves the camera being placed in a confined space.

■ *e.g.* a shot taken from inside a cupboard as the subject opens the cupboard door

**crane shot:** a type of shot in which a camera is positioned on a specially designed crane, which can be raised and lowered at will.

■ A crane shot is a high-angle shot but the versatility of the equipment allows a director to start a shot from a high angle and then swoop down toward a subject at ground level.

**crawler:** the line of moving text that runs across the bottom of the television screen during a news broadcast on dedicated news channels like CNN.

**creative team:** the individuals employed by an advertising agency with responsibility for thinking up and designing a campaign strategy.

■ Their remit will usually include devising slogans and campaign themes, making sketches and drawing up storyboards for presentation to clients.

**crew:** the individuals responsible for elements of an audio-visual production.
■ *e.g.* sound crew, camera crew, film crew

**crime fiction:** important television genre, dating from the 1950s and encompassing a whole range of programmes, with narratives and representations adapted to reflect changing social and cultural values and expectations.

■ Crime-fiction drama exists in many varied forms, ranging from the traditional 'whodunnit' detective story (e.g. Agatha Christie's *Poirot* and Colin Dexter's *Inspector Morse*) to hard-hitting contemporary dramas (e.g. Jimmy McGovern's *Cracker*, 1993). Consequently, it appeals to many different audiences.

■ **Representations** of the police and criminals have varied considerably since the 1950s, with British **mainstream** series such as *Dixon of Dock Green, Z-Cars, The Sweeny* and *The Bill* attempting 'realistic' domestic **representations** of crime and law-and-order issues, with **narratives** reflecting the changing British social scene. Such series can act as vehicles for the airing of public concerns over crime and related issues and the nature of consensual policing, sometimes with a **social-action** agenda, e.g. drug abuse, domestic violence, juvenile crime, alcohol-related crime, racism and even police corruption.

■ ***TIP*** Imported US series, ranging from *Dragnet* (1950s and a contemporary remake) to *NYPD Blue* (1990s–), have always provided more escapist entertainment value, representing a different crime culture and distant locations.

**critical autonomy:** the ability to research a topic, to assess and evaluate evidence and to come to an informed, personal judgement.

■ ***TIP*** In media studies, a demonstration of critical autonomy is important.

**cropping:** the practice of cutting and trimming photographs for publication in newspapers and magazines, either to fit available space or to emphasise or alter key elements of the image.

■ Cropping can distort the original context of a photograph by enlarging some features and omitting others.

■ The term is also used in the context of film.

**crosscut:** a type of moving image edit that involves a series of **cutaways** and cutbacks from one sequence of **narrative** action to another taking place simultaneously.

■ ***e.g.*** The closing scenes of *The Godfather Part III* (Francis Ford Coppola, 1990) involve cutting between five **parallel-action** narrative sequences, including a stage opera which provides the musical backdrop to the whole action. The result is to raise the level of dramatic intensity and tension.

**cross genre:** see hybrid.

**cross-media ownership:** the practice of a single corporation having business interests in several different types of media.

■ ***e.g.*** News Corporation owns areas of the press and of television and film production and distribution.

**CRT:** see cathode-ray tube.

**cultivation theory:** audience research in the **effects theory** tradition, begun by George **Gerbner** in the 1960s.

■ Gerbner conducted research on how watching television affects people's views of the real world. Cultivation theorists argue that television has long-term effects, which are small, gradual, indirect, cumulative and ultimately significant.

■ Television tends to reinforce values already present in a culture and to support the dominant ideology. Cultivation research also focuses on exposure to violence and sex and whether or not this can be said to influence viewers.

■ Cultivation theory is in the passive rather than active audience theory tradition and, unlike more recent developments in the effects approach, does not allow for an oppositional reading by the viewer or for the audience's attitudes, beliefs and values to influence the way they interpret media content. The increasingly varied range of output and the growing emphasis on the choices made by an active viewer also challenge Gerbner's approach.

**cultural capital:** term devised by the French sociologist Pierre Bourdieu (1930–2002) in 1977 to describe the range of cultural competences which are transmitted to middle-class children, via their parents, and which enable them to make the best use of the education system.

■ *TIP* The concept is useful in media research since it helps to explain how different audiences respond in different ways to the same media text.

**cultural competence:** term used by French sociologist Pierre Bourdieu (1930–2002) to describe the advantage given to middle-class children in the education system as a result of their parental and cultural background.

**cultural effects theory:** audience theory which argues that, in the absence of real substantial evidence of the direct relationship between media texts and people's behaviour, the effects of exposure to the media should be seen as long term and more subtle. Unlike cultivation theory, the effects approach increasingly focuses on the different ways in which audiences respond to media content.

■ Constant exposure to particular messages can be seen as slowly affecting judgement and attitudes in the same way that the constant dripping of water from a tap wears away a stone. Cultural effects theory is associated with Stuart Hall and a Marxist approach to the part played by media content in reinforcing dominant ideology, in particular in relation to race and gender issues.

■ In some cases, audiences may accept the preferred readings of polysemic media messages without challenging them, while other audiences may resist texts with oppositional readings. Negotiated readings, where audiences partially accept texts, represent a compromise between these positions.

**cultural imperialism:** the dominance of Western, particularly US, cultural values and ideology across the world.

■ Cultural imperialism is a growing issue, with globalisation and the increasing domination of world media output by a few giant companies. This is combined with the tendency of the dominant culture to absorb texts generated by other cultures and to reproduce them in its own image.

■ *e.g.* The Spanish film *Open Your Eyes* (Alejandro Amenábar, 1997) was remade with Tom Cruise in a US context as *Vanilla Sky* (Cameron Crowe, 2001); the Japanese horror film *Ring* (Hideo Nakata, 1998) was remade in the USA as *The Ring* by DreamWorks (Gore Verbinski, 2002).

**cultural transmission:** the process through which symbolic structures and dominant discourses characteristic of a social group or culture are passed from one generation to another.
■ Marxists would argue that this process ensures the reproduction of the cultural values of the dominant class, particularly through the education system and the mass media.

**culture:** the social practices of a group of people, usually involving shared language, history, values, beliefs, lifestyle, appearance, dress and entertainment.
■ The relative merits of different aspects of culture and subculture and the key role played by the media in the representation of cultural values and cultural reproduction are the focus of intense debate.

**culture industry:** a term used by Theodor Adorno, a member of the Frankfurt School, who saw mass culture as an industry produced and controlled by capitalism for the benefit of the ruling elite.
■ Adorno argues that the culture industry is used systematically to manipulate the masses via the media to ensure their continuing obedience to market interests and to neutralise any dissenting views (e.g. youth cultures) by a process of incorporation. Individuals are unable to resist the constant prepared diet of media texts and, as victims of mass deception, are incapable of independent thought and unaware of their true socioeconomic circumstances. Popular culture is seen as shallow and dehumanising.
■ *TIP* Look for elements of this highly pessimistic view of human cultural experience in dystopian science-fiction films such as *The Matrix* and *The Matrix Reloaded* (Wachowski Brothers, 1999 and 2003).

**Cumberbatch, Guy:** director of the communications research group at Aston University, Birmingham (2005), and a prominent researcher into the effects of sex and violence on media audiences.
■ Cumberbatch has reviewed much of the work in this field and found in many cases that the research base did not justify the findings, particularly where claims of damaging effects had been made. His approach is consistently sceptical about far-reaching claims made on the basis of limited and questionable data.

**cut:** a type of moving image editing in which one image changes directly into another. A cut is the commonest form of continuity editing.

**cutaway:** a brief shot that momentarily interrupts the main action of a film by showing a related action, object or person, not necessarily part of the main scene, before cutting back to the original shot.

■ Often filmed from the point of view of one of the characters, a cutaway provides visual relief, eases transition from one shot to another, breaks up a sequence and provides information on or hints at impending changes. Reaction shots are usually edited as cutaways. See crosscut.

**cyberculture:** the notion that use of the internet creates new patterns of interaction and new forms of cultural relationship between participants who have never met.

**cyberpunk:** a film genre variant developed from literature, a cross between science fiction and contemporary street culture, set in a joyless dystopian world where machines, technology and large corporations control people's lives.

■ Resistance is often in the form of an underground or subversive popular culture.

■ *e.g.* *Metropolis* (Fritz Lang, 1927) was the first film in the genre, followed by *Blade Runner* (Ridley Scott, 1982), *The Fifth Element* (Luc Besson, 1997), *Brazil* (Terry Gilliam, 1985), *Terminator 2* (James Cameron, 1991), *The Matrix* (Wachowski Brothers, 1999).

**cyborg:** a fictional hybrid combination of a machine and an organism (usually human).

■ The cyborg reflects the development of microtechnologies in the late twentieth century and the consequent breakdown of the boundaries between organism and machine. It also reflects the increasing fluidity in roles and identities characteristic of the postmodern world.

■ *e.g.* the Borg in *Star Trek: First Contact* (Jonathan Frakes, 1996)

**DAB (digital audio broadcasting):** see radio.

*Daily Express*: tabloid national daily newspaper with right-of-centre politics, published by Express Newspapers.

■ The *Daily Express*, founded in 1900, was the first newspaper to carry news instead of adverts on the front page. Acquired by Max Aitken (later Lord Beaverbrook) in 1916, by 1936 it had a circulation of 2.25 million copies, the largest in the world at that time.

■ Circulation wars with the politically opposing *Daily Mirror* dominated the 1950s, with circulations then standing at over 4 million. Beaverbrook died in 1964 and the Beaverbrook family finally sold the declining title in 1985 to United Newspapers (now United Business Media).

■ Continuing decline and uncertain politics meant that the paper was unable to match the growing success of its long-term rival the *Daily Mail*, and the group was bought by Richard Desmond's Northern and Shell company in 2000. Circulation was down to 949,238 copies in January 2005.

*Daily Mail*: tabloid national daily newspaper with right-of-centre politics.

■ First published in 1896 and devised by Lords Northcliffe and Rothermere, the *Daily Mail* is still owned by the same Harmsworth family, as part of Associated Newspapers.

■ The paper has a long tradition of supporting right-of-centre politics — in the late 1930s, under the then owner, Lord Rothermere, it advocated the avoidance of war by appeasement of Hitler.

■ Strongly anti-European and supportive of the Thatcher government in the 1980s, the paper became the established voice of middle England and the aspiring middle classes.

■ Its successful formula saw off its rival the *Daily Express*. Its circulation stood at 2,409,121 in January 2005, second only to the *Sun* in UK daily tabloid sales.

**Daily Mirror:** New-Labour supporting, centre-left national daily **tabloid** newspaper, owned by **Mirror Group Newspapers** (MGN), part of **Trinity Mirror,** the largest UK newspaper publisher.

■ The *Daily Mirror* was founded in 1903 as part of the Northcliffe/Rothermere publishing empire, which included the *Daily Mail.* During the 1950s, it was run by Rothermere's nephew Cecil Harmsworth King, chairman of Mirror Newspapers Ltd, and as a classic **red top** tabloid, it reached a circulation of 4.5 million during this decade.

■ Mirror Newspapers became part of **IPC Media** in 1963 and then of Reed International in 1970. It faced strong competition from Rupert Murdoch's *Sun* during the 1970s and 1980s and its circulation fell. In 1984, the group was acquired by corrupt tycoon Robert Maxwell for what became a disastrous period in its history. MGN survived Maxwell's death and disgrace in 1991 to be taken over by Trinity to form the Trinity Mirror group in 1999.

■ The *Daily Mirror's* circulation has fallen from its heyday in the 1950s (1,748,327 copies, January 2005).

**Daily Telegraph:** daily quality **broadsheet** newspaper, with the largest circulation for its format (920,745 copies, January 2005).

■ The *Telegraph* is a conservative-supporting newspaper with, traditionally, a strong middle-class readership. Its circulation is not as healthy as it seems, however, since it suffers from an ageing readership, which deters advertisers. Its rival *The Times* now sells more full price copies (*Daily Telegraph* figures are boosted by discounted subscription sales).

■ Acquired in 2004 by the Barclay Brothers, following a protracted wrangle with the former owner Lord Black, the paper faces some difficult decisions on its future direction.

**day-for-night:** a filming technique where shots taken in daylight, using special filters, lighting and the underexposure of film, are used as night-time shots in the finished product.

■ *e.g. Day for Night* (François Truffaut, 1973), *The Day of the Locust* (John Schlesinger, 1975)

**dead donkey:** a trivial, inconsequential news item used as a filler in news programmes, often involving animals, and easily pushed off the agenda by the advent of more important stories.

**decoding model:** see encoding/decoding model.

**deconstruction:** the process of taking a text apart to explore and analyse its component elements, originally developed in the 1960s by French academic Jacques Derrida (1930–2004).

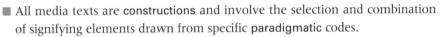

- All media texts are **constructions** and involve the selection and combination of signifying elements drawn from specific **paradigmatic** codes.
- Deconstruction is a key principle of **semiological** analysis and is used to explain how the combination of **signs** in any text are used to create meaning.

**deep focus:** a camera technique that allows objects both near and far from the camera to be in focus at the same time.

**demographics:** information concerning the social status, class, gender and age of the population.
- Audience profiles use demographic information, the best-known system being the ABC1 scale.

**demonisation:** sensational media reporting that turns individuals or groups into folk devils and makes them the focus of **moral panic** by distorting and exaggerating their actions and behaviour.
- *e.g.* Supporters of Millwall Football Club have a media-generated reputation for excessive violence and bad behaviour.

**denotation:** the first and simplest level of meaning of an image.
- *e.g.* A picture of a rose represents the rose flower and reminds the viewer of the real thing.

**denouement (from the French for 'unknotting'):** the unravelling and explanation of a plot at the end of a dramatic **narrative**.
- *e.g.* Agatha Christie's fictional detective Hercule Poirot often brings all the characters together in the denouement to identify the murderer and to explain how he has solved the crime.

**Department of Agitation and Propaganda:** see agitprop.

**dependency theory:** a passive audience theory associated with researchers Sandra Ball-Rokeach and Melvin DeFleur, focusing on the degree to which audiences become dependent on the media.
- The researchers argue that the greater the uncertainty there is in a society, the more audiences will become dependent on media communication to form judgements and make sense of the world.
- *TIP* Although it is obvious that most people depend on the media for knowledge of news and events outside their immediate experience, the approach probably underestimates the extent to which audience members will form negotiated or alternative readings of texts, other than those intended, in line with their own experience, attitudes, beliefs and values.

**deregulation:** the changes in the state regulation of broadcasting that resulted from of the **Broadcasting Act of 1990**, the **Broadcasting Act of 1996** and the more recent Communications Act of 2003, all of which progressively allowed much greater competition and less regulation among a larger number of broad-casting organisations.

■ Deregulation was the result of considerable pressure from commercial media organisations and also of developments in technology, which meant that satellite coverage of western Europe by independent commercial operators challenged the regulatory systems of individual nation states. The result was a considerable increase in available television channels and the relaxing of prescriptive legislation.

■ Critics of television deregulation argue that the move was a political act insomuch as it changed the content and scope of programming by moving away from a **public service broadcasting** model toward a more market-orientated model, involving formulaic entertainment, less challenging news, documentaries and cheaply made fillers.

**determinism:** the **Marxist** concept that individuals and institutions have no choice in their behaviour because their decisions are shaped by socioeconomic forces beyond their control.

■ Determinism sees the media as dominated by the economic interests of political and social **elites**, with the ideology of these elites shaping and determining the content of media texts.

■ *TIP* Contrast this view with **pluralism** which argues that the large number of media institutions and products available provides audiences with a wide freedom of choice.

**deviance:** behaviour that 'deviates' (turns away) from the **norm** or that which is generally accepted within a society.

■ Norm-referenced behaviour is seen as supporting **dominant ideology**. Media products that challenge **dominant ideology** are often accused of encouraging deviant behaviour, particularly in relation to teenagers.

■ *e.g.* *The Wild One* (Laslo Benedek, 1953) was banned for causing teddy-boy riots; *Rock around the Clock* (Fred F. Sears, 1956) was blamed for cinemas being defaced by teddy boys; *A Clockwork Orange* (Stanley Kubrick, 1971) was blamed for an increase in teenage gang violence and **copy cat** killings; *Natural Born Killers* (Oliver Stone, 1994) was accused of causing copy cat killings.

■ *TIP* The perceived relationship between deviant behaviour and media texts has often led to **moral panic** reactions and demands for the banning of particular films.

**diachronic:** in narrative, describing events that move through time sequentially.

■ Diachronic is the opposite of **synchronic** which means at the same time.

■ Both terms are useful for describing the way film makers use time sequences to construct narrative.

■ *e.g.* the television series *24*

**diegesis:** the story-line or narrative which includes the whole fictional world created by a media text.

**diegetic sound:** sound generated within a film narrative.
- Non-diegetic sound is outside the narrative such as an orchestra playing rousing music during a battle scene.
- *e.g.* the sound of traffic in a scene involving a road

**digital:** describes a communication system that is based on the storage and retrieval of numerical information.
- The digital revolution involves the application of digital technology to all aspects of telecommunications and television reception, with a government objective of digitalisation of all television signals and the replacement of analogue by 2012.

**digital audio broadcasting (DAB):** see radio.

**digital television:** sound and images that are converted to computerised digits for reception by aerials, satellites or cables and then decoded in a television set top box.
- The system is faster, allows for multiple channels and produces better-quality images than the analogue signal. Digital signals also allow for greater interaction with pay-per-view television, television shopping and choices of viewing angles already available to viewers.

**digital versatile (video) disk (DVD):** a compact digital storage device that uses compression to allow feature films or computer data to be carried on one disk.

**director:** the individual responsible for the overall creation of a film, including the *mise en scène*, and the structuring of individual shots, and with artistic control over the film's final appearance, including the way in which it is edited and constructed.
- The extent of a director's control over a film is subject to the contractual terms under which the production is financed and to any controlling interest left with the financial backers. Directors and financiers may find themselves in conflict where commercial and artistic values are incompatible.
- *e.g.* Italian director Bernardo Bertolucci's epic film *1900* (1976), about the history of Italy in the twentieth century, was savagely cut by the film's US backers and divided into two separate parts. It was only finally restored in 1995.

**director's cut:** an edited alternative version of a commercial film where the film director has total control over the editing process.
- The director's cut is often seen as having greater artistic merit than the standard commercial version of a film since it is the work of an individual with overall

artistic control. This is particularly important where the director is seen as an auteur with a distinctive, identifiable personal style.

■ *e.g. Blade Runner* (Ridley Scott, director's cut, 1993), *Donnie Darko* (Richard Kelly, director's cut, 2004)

**disaster movie:** film genre that focuses on a disaster scenario.

■ Disaster movies usually have a simple equilibrium/disequilibrium/equilibrium narrative and fairly thinly drawn characters. Their main audience appeal is the build-up to the disaster and the subsequent destruction that follows. Aimed at mainstream audiences, they are heavy on special effects and light on screenplay and plot development.

■ Disasters can include: earthquakes, tornados, sinking ships, burning skyscrapers, volcanic eruptions and, more recently, meteor threats to the planet and global warming. The excitement of disaster movies formed popular escapism when the social climate was stable and secure. More recent versions reflect current fears over threats to the world order and climate change, although the mood after 9/11 has reinforced a general decline in the genre's popularity.

■ *e.g.* Classic examples include *The Poseidon Adventure* (Ronald Neame, 1972), *Earthquake* (Mark Robson, 1974) and *Towering Inferno* (John Guillerman, 1974). More recent variants include *Twister* (Jan de Bont, 1996), *Titanic* (James Cameron, 1997), *Volcano* (Mick Jackson, 1997), *Armageddon* (Michael Bay, 1998) and *The Day After Tomorrow* (Roland Emmerich, 2004).

**discourse:** the agreed terms of reference framing the discussion of social, economic and personal relationships in a society.

■ All social and media debates take place within an agreed value system, using accepted terms of reference, and this can act as a constraint and limitation on what can be discussed and how events and phenomena are interpreted.

■ Newspapers construct discourses around the assumed beliefs and values of their readership, with certain elements taken for granted. For example, readers are expected to be shocked or disturbed by murders, sexual misconduct and football violence. It is difficult for readers to challenge the assumed point of view.

■ Media discourses can be constructed from alternative points of view. For example, the controversial film *Kids* (Larry Clark, 1995) was constructed from within the adolescent community and showed the kids breaking every 'under age' rule in relation to sex, drugs and general behaviour. It shocked and disturbed adult audiences. Catherine Hardwicke's film *Thirteen* (2003) covered similar ground but with less sensationalism.

**disequilibrium:** the disruption of narrative by persons or events presenting a challenge to the harmonious equilibrium often found at the beginning of a film or other media text.

- Disequilibrium is an important device for sustaining the interest of readers or viewers who will seek resolution through a restoration of equilibrium in the **denouement** and so maintain their interest in the text.
- See Tzvetan **Todorov**'s narrative theory.

**Disney Corporation (the Walt Disney Company):** a vertically integrated, diversified, international media corporation founded by Walt **Disney**.

- The company has wide holdings across media industries including publishing, broadcasting, film, multimedia, music, theatre, sports and theme parks.
- Disney companies include: ABC Television (USA) and US regional television holdings, the History Channel, the Disney Channel (worldwide), Buena Vista Television, Touchstone Television, Walt Disney Pictures, **Touchstone Pictures**, Hollywood Pictures, Caravan Pictures, **Miramax**, Buena Vista International, together with internet, music, sports and Disneyland theme parks.

**Disney, Walt (1901–66):** the founder of the Disney media and entertainment organisation and creator of Mickey Mouse, Donald Duck and Goofy.

- Walt Disney developed cartoon animation and produced the first full-length colour feature cartoon film, *Snow White and the Seven Dwarfs* (David Hand, 1937). This was followed by *Fantasia* (Ben Sharpsteen, 1940), *Bambi* (David Hand, 1942), *Cinderella* (Wilfred Jackson, 1950) and *Peter Pan* (Hamilton Luske, Clyde Geronimi and Wilfred Jackson, 1953).
- The characters created by Disney and the imaginary, fairy tale world they inhabited gave rise to his concept of the theme park world of Disneyland, first opened in California in 1955 with associated merchandising of Disney characters and lifestyle.
- Critics of Disney see his recasting of the world's heritage of fairy and folk tales in a US mould (**Disneyfication**) as a classic example of **cultural imperialism**, and his theme parks as simulated reality or **simulacra**.
- Recent Disney animation successes using **computer-generated imagery** technology include *Beauty and the Beast* (Gary Trousdale, 1991) and *Monsters, Inc.* (Peter Docter, 2001) in association with **Pixar**. However, Disney's agreement with Pixar has since ended and there has been considerable boardroom disagreement as to the future direction of the company.
- *TIP* The Disney label is associated with wholesome family entertainment and Disney uses its subsidiary company **Touchstone Pictures** to front products with a slightly more adult content.

**Disneyfication:** a term used by critics of the Disney style to describe the way in which a story is sanitised by the removal of controversial sexual, morally ambivalent, or violent content in order to make it suitable for family viewing. Disneyfication also involves the neutralising of cultural differences and variations, either through the creation of safe ethnic stereotypes or their elimination from the narrative altogether.

■ *e.g.* *Pocahontas* (Mike Gabriel and Eric Goldberg, 1995), a pro-colonial narrative with stereotyped ethnicity and patriarchal values. The genocidal behaviour of early white settlers in their conduct towards Native Americans is conveniently sanitised.

**dissolve:** a type of moving image editing where one image slowly dissolves into another.

**distributor:** the company or organisation responsible for buying a film from the producers and distributing it.

■ Distribution companies are often subdivisions of major media and film-production conglomerates, such as Twentieth Century Fox and Warner Brothers, which in some countries (not Britain) also control the multiplex cinemas where most people see films. Their choices are entirely determined by commercial considerations. Efficient distribution is a major factor in the success or failure of a film and a few large companies effectively act as gatekeepers controlling the market; if executives don't like a film, it doesn't get released.

■ Small independent producers need to find smaller distributors interested in their product to ensure it gets exposure to audiences. Timed internet, digital versatile (video) disk, cable, rental and sale release of the product are increasingly seen as an all-in-one solution, whereby independent producers can bypass gatekeepers and find an audience.

■ *TIP* Film release can be controversial: Disney, owners of Miramax film distributors, attempted to block the release of Michael Moore's politically controversial film *Fahrenheit 9/11* (2004) raising questions of political gatekeeping and censorship.

**documentary:** any film made about real life as opposed to being a fictional construct.

■ Although documentaries are sometimes regarded as neutral observations of life, they are in fact subject to the same process of construction and editorial control as any other film. Pioneer documentary maker John Grierson described documentary as 'the creative treatment of actuality' and commented: 'Documentary is not a mirror which reflects society but a hammer with which to shape it.' See docusoap, drama documentary, realism.

**docusoap:** a television genre that combines elements of soap opera with documentary and focuses on the lives of real people. See also fly-on-the-wall.

■ *e.g.* *Airport, Driving School*

**dominant ideology:** the belief system that serves the interests of the dominant ruling elite within a society, generally accepted as common sense by the majority and reproduced in mainstream media texts.

- Dominant ideology establishes a **hegemonic** position in society which is reinforced by media representations and is consequently difficult to challenge.
- The term derives from **Marxist** theory and is addressed in detail in the work of Gramsci, **Althusser** and **Hall**.

**dominant (or hegemonic) reading:** a response to a text in which the reader shares the value system of the text and accepts the preferred reading without question.

- The term was introduced by Stuart **Hall** and developed by David **Morley** as part of his *Nationwide* study (1980) (see **reception theory**).

**door-stepping:** the journalistic practice of seeking to interview or confront individuals in the public eye, either by ambushing them unexpectedly in a public place or by visiting them unannounced at home, usually with a camera crew, in the hope of obtaining an unrehearsed, spontaneous response to awkward questions.

- Apart from being a direct method of forcing people to face questions which are arguably in the **public interest**, door-stepping makes good television and radio material because of the excitement generated by the unpredictability of the outcome and the confrontational nature of the encounters.
- *e.g.* *The Cook Report* (Roger Cook, ITV, 1980s–90s)

**drama documentary:** a television **documentary** that takes the form of a drama based on actual events, thus blurring the distinction between fiction and reality and attracting a wider audience by raising the entertainment value of the content.

- *e.g.* *Bloody Sunday* (Charles McDougall and Jimmy McGovern, Gaslight Productions, 2002, Channel 4)

**DreamWorks:** digital-animation film and television production and distribution company founded by Steven Spielberg, Jeffrey Katzenburg and David Geffen in 1994, a rival to **Disney** and producer of *Shrek* and *Shrek 2* (Andrew Adamson, 2001 and 2004).

**dumbing down:** the practice of reducing the intellectual or academic content of a media or cultural text in order to make it accessible to a larger audience.

- The term is used disparagingly by those who disapprove of the popularisation of media content and see it as part of a decline in programme quality.
- *e.g.* Producers of simplified or popularised versions of Shakespeare's plays or Chaucer's texts are often accused of dumbing down, e.g. *William Shakespeare's Romeo + Juliet* (Baz Luhrmann, 1996), which was aimed at a teenage audience and criticised by some, but praised by others for its relevant and original contemporary treatment. In television news, the inclusion of more human-interest stories and less **hard news** is also seen as dumbing down.

**Dutch angle (also known as 'canted shot'):** a type of camera shot which involves tilting the camera to create a sense of disorientation.

**DVD:** see digital versatile (video) disk.

**dystopia:** a dysfunctional, pessimistic view of the world gone wrong (often set in the future), where tyranny, disease, bad technology, alien invasion, oppression, environmental disaster or other catastrophes are seen to befall humankind.

■ In film, dystopian narratives are extensions of the science-fiction/action genre and often extend and expand existing conditions to heighten the sense of realism. See cyberpunk.

■ *e.g.* *Blade Runner* (Ridley Scott, 1982), *The Terminator* (James Cameron, 1984), *Armageddon* (Michael Bay, 1998), *The Matrix* (Wachowski Brothers, 1999), *28 Days Later* (Danny Boyle, 2002)

**Ealing Studios:** a film studio established at Ealing, London, in 1931, most famous for a series of low-budget, distinctly British comedies in the immediate postwar period.

■ Headed by Michael Balcon, 1937–58, the studio is associated with a famous generation of British actors including Alec Guinness and Stanley Holloway. It was sold to the BBC in 1955 and finally closed in 1958.

■ *e.g.* *Passport to Pimlico* (Henry Cornelius, 1949), *The Lavender Hill Mob* (Charles Crichton, 1951), *The Titfield Thunderbolt* (Charles Crichton, 1953), *The Ladykillers* (Alexander Mackendrick, 1955)

**edit:** the selection and construction of the various elements that form a completed media text.

**editor:** the person responsible for the content of a newspaper or magazine.

■ Editors take decisions concerning content, style and the point of view adopted by their publication and are ultimately held responsible for any failings, mistakes or errors of judgement.

■ Editors are often described as gatekeepers because they have the power to decide what is and what is not included in media texts.

■ *e.g.* Piers Morgan was sacked as editor of the *Daily Mirror* in 2004 for an error of judgement in publishing fake photographs purporting to show the abuse of Iraqi prisoners by British soldiers during the 2003 Iraq War. Bruce Yelland was sacked as editor of the *Sun* for failing to maintain its circulation figures.

**editorial:** an article or column written by the editor of a newspaper or magazine, reflecting the positioning of that publication in relation to politics, issues of the day and its particular remit.

■ *e.g.* *Farmer's Weekly* editorials are likely to be concerned with the impact of political decisions on farming, whereas *Sight and Sound* editorials will be concerned with media policy and film finance.

**editorialising:** the journalistic practice, commonly exercised by radio and television news presenters, of making summarising and judgemental comments, preceding or following a broadcast item, which often include an evaluative point of view.

■ Critics argue that in using their authority in this way presenters are influencing the audience's response to the item in question.

■ *e.g.* In the aftermath of the 2003 Iraq War and following the death of government scientific expert Dr David Kelly, BBC Radio 4 *Today* reporter Andrew Gilligan claimed that Kelly had implied that the government had 'sexed up' a controversial dossier on Iraq's weapons of mass destruction in order to persuade Parliament to support the war. Gilligan made his comments during a live discussion of a meeting he had held with Kelly and the phrase 'sexed up' was picked up and used by commentators when discussing the issue. The comments were the centre of a public row between the BBC and the government on the limits of journalistic licence and the importance of balanced reporting.

**effects theory:** an audience theory that tends to see the audience as passive and seeks to measure how exposure to particular aspects of media content can influence the behaviour of the reader or viewer.

■ In traditional effects theory, the audience is influenced by media content in negative ways, resulting in effects that are often regarded as problematic in terms of threatening social stability. The theory helps explain moral panic responses to media content, particularly in relation to representations of sex, violence and deviant behaviour and its supposed effects on youth.

■ Critics of television content such as Mary Whitehouse are essentially in the effects tradition.

■ Hypodermic theory is the earliest and simplest effects model but empirical evidence to support its claims has always been difficult to obtain. Cultivation theory belongs to the same tradition, with the emphasis shifting from immediate to more gradual, ideological effects.

■ Objective evidence to assess the effects of the media on audiences is difficult to gather and assess. Critics like Guy Cumberbatch argue that studies are often devised in such a way as to justify the opinion of the researcher and that there is a serious shortage of valid objective evidence.

**elite:** a small select group in a society which claims leadership privileges as a result of expertise, in terms of knowledge or skill, in a particular field.

■ Elites exist in broadcasting institutions where they determine programme content and representations.

■ In terms of audiences, elites may be viewed as sought-after niche markets.

■ Elitism is the practice of separating from the mass through claims of specialist knowledge or ability.

**ellipsis:** the removal or shortening of elements of a narrative to speed up the action.

■ In film, this is made acceptable to audiences through editing techniques, such as scene change, dissolve or fade.

**Emap:** a newspaper company founded in 1947, now a major UK media organisation and the biggest digital operator in the UK, with 150 consumer magazines, 19 analogue radio stations and seven digital radio stations.
■ Emap is the second-largest UK magazine publisher, with 16% of the market share. It is currently competing with IPC Media for lead position in the men's weekly market, with *Zoo Weekly* competing against IPC's *Nuts*.
■ In 2004, Emap closed two well-known but failing titles, *J-17* and *The Face*.
■ Current titles include *Bliss*, *Kerrang*, *More*, *Heat*, *Red*, *Smash Hits*, *Zoo Weekly* and *FHM*.

**embedded journalist:** a journalist working alongside a military unit in a combat zone.
■ Embedded journalists accept some limitations on their activities and possibly in some cases on their editorial freedom in return for a relatively safe and privileged front-line, eye-witness position.
■ *e.g.* In the 2003 Iraq War, many journalists were embedded with US and British forces (e.g. the BBC's Gavin Hewitt and Andrew Harding).
■ *TIP* The practice has caused concern over the impartiality of the reporting since embedded journalists can be seen as mouthpieces for the military units in which they are placed.

**empathy:** the ability to share the emotions or point of view of a group or individual.
■ Empathy involves recognising shared experience rather than sympathising from a detached position.
■ Human-interest journalism, feature writing and reality television often involve emotionally identifying the reader/viewer with the subject, with the intention of thereby sustaining audience interest.

**Empire:** monthly film magazine launched at the Cannes Film Festival in 1989.

**empiricism:** method of research based on the measuring and testing of observable evidence.
■ *e.g.* content analysis
■ *TIP* Media research based on empirical evidence often claims scientific status, such as the Bobo doll experiment into the effects of children being exposed to media violence. Closer examination of research methods and results can sometimes reveal biased, limited or ambiguous criteria which are then used by researchers to form exaggerated, far-reaching and unjustifiable conclusions.

**encode:** the process of constructing a media message in a form suitable for transmission to a receiver or target audience.

**encoding/decoding model:** model devised by Stuart Hall to explore the ways in which the meanings of media texts can vary in line with their circumstances of production and consumption.

**enigma code:** a narrative structure that involves the creation of riddles or problems to be solved by the resolution.
- Suspense and horror genres use enigma to retain the attention of an audience.

**epic:** a film produced on a large scale with a large cast, impressive settings and locations and a powerful theme, often involving life-and-death power struggles, love, conflict and tragedy.
- Epics are big-budget films and can be from any genre. They are distinguished by their scale of production.
- Common themes include biblical and historical events.
- *e.g.* *Gone with the Wind* (Victor Fleming, 1939), *Ben Hur* (William Wyler, 1959), *Gladiator* (Ridley Scott, 2000)

**equilibrium:** the harmonious state that often exists at the start of a narrative before disruptive or transforming elements are introduced. See Todorov.

**Equity:** see Actors' Equity Association.

**establishment:** the institutions of monarchy, the church, the higher civil service and the higher judiciary, formerly seen as consisting of an influential, unelected, wealthy, ruling elite.
- With the increased democratisation of society and the opening up of closed professions, it could be argued that the term has begun to lose its significance.
- In the past the media have been seen as upholding the interests of the establishment, e.g. in the late 1930s all the world knew of Edward VIII's love affair with Wallace Simpson except people in Britain, where press barons had agreed to keep the affair secret.
- *TIP* Marxists see the establishment as upholding dominant ideology reinforced by the media.

**ethnography:** a form of research where the researcher attempts to understand a culture by becoming part of it.
- Ethnographers attempt to live the lives of the cultures they study, using audio tape or written notes to record their findings.
- *e.g.* In his audience research, David Morley spent several weeks living with households and watching television with family members.
- *TIP* Critics of ethnography argue that it can be difficult for the researcher both to detach his/her own values from the study and to avoid speaking from a prepared position on behalf of those whose views are being researched.

**ethnomethodology:** a qualitative, empiricist research method used in reception theory and based on explanations of experiences constructed by the participants themselves through group discussion.

■ By allowing the researched to speak for themselves, this method avoids the interpretive academic overview, usually provided by the researcher, which can influence findings.

**evaluation:** an assessment of the strengths and weaknesses of a piece of work by the individual responsible for producing it, as measured against the brief or other set of criteria used in its construction..

■ *TIP* Depending on the course specification, an evaluation can be presented as a separate piece of work or as part of a larger log, and is essential in establishing how decisions were made, under what circumstances and with what outcomes. Evaluations should be objective and should involve self-criticism where necessary. They should be an honest assessment of a finished piece of work, measured against its original aims and objectives.

***Evening Standard:*** regional newspaper for the London area, owned by Associated Newspapers, the publishers of the *Daily Mail.*

**exclusive:** a story line unique to a particular broadcaster or publication.

■ In an increasingly competitive media environment, there is considerable pressure on broadcasters and newspaper editors to generate exclusive stories that grab public attention away from their rivals (see cheque book journalism).

**expressionism:** an early twentieth-century art movement in which dramatic personal and emotional self-expression is the keynote of artworks.

■ In cinema, it is associated with films made in Germany just after the First World War, which involve heavily exaggerated, emotional and melodramatic characters, strongly contrasting use of light and shade (chiaroscuro), dramatic surrealist sets, tilted Dutch angles and often futuristic settings.

■ *The Cabinet of Dr Caligari* (Robert Wiene, 1919) was the first expressionist film widely seen outside Germany.

■ *Nosferatu* (F. W. Murnau, 1922) has strong expressionist elements with sharp-edged sets, chiaroscuro lighting and the vampire as a shadowy creature with rodent features.

■ *Metropolis* (Fritz Lang, 1927) has strong expressionist influences.

**eyeline match:** a type of editing that maintains the eyeline or level when cutting from a character to what the character sees.

■ The effect of the edit is to create a sense that what the camera sees is what the character sees.

**fabulation:** the construction of moralising stories about the origins of conflict in a society and the positive resolution of that conflict.
- Fabulation involves the construction of allegorical narrative where characters are used to act out a particular example of a dilemma which then becomes a metonym for larger social issues. The resolution reinforces the mainstream values of the society involved and overlooks underlying contradictions.
- *e.g.* *The Patriot* (Roland Emmerich, 2000), *Pearl Harbor* (Michael Bay, 2001)
- *TIP* War movies are a useful vehicle for melodramatic fabulation.

**fade:** a type of moving image editing where the image gradually fades and disappears, leaving a white or black screen.

**false consciousness:** Marxist term for the effect of dominant ideology on the awareness of workers with regard to their real economic and social circumstances.
- Marxists argue that workers are manipulated by institutions, such as the education system, organised religion and the mass media, and are unaware of their unequal status and exploitation by capitalism.

**family values:** traditional conservative beliefs associated with mainstream political and religious views of society.
- Family values are often represented as being under threat from alien, subversive or immoral forces. These forces can include ethnic minorities, extremist political groupings, youth cultures such as punks and goths, music such as rap and pornography. Family values are often cited as being the core ideology of newspapers such as the *Daily Mail*, which appeals to a traditional, middle-class, mainstream audience.

**fantasy:** genre built around an artificially constructed reality which could never exist in real life, often involving classical mythology or fairy tale.
- Fantasy films generally set real human characters against mythical or super-natural creatures in an imaginary world.
- Computer-generated images have made possible a dramatic extension of the fantasy universe.

■ *e.g.* The Seventh Voyage of Sinbad (Nathan Juran, 1958), *Jason and the Argonauts* (Don Chaffey, 1963), *Willow* (Ron Howard, 1988), *The Lord of the Rings* trilogy (Peter Jackson, 2001–03)

**farce:** light-hearted, crude, exaggerated comedy, usually involving the satirising of a stock situation, often through the embarrassment and comic humiliation of characters.

**feature (1):** the principal film shown in a cinema.
■ In the 1940s and 1950s, feature films were supported by a second **B-movie** in order to offer good value to cinema-goers.

**feature (2):** an article in a newspaper concerned with a topical issue and with no **hard news** content.

**feedback:** any mechanism or communication that is designed to reduce the gap between intended and actual performance.
■ Feedback is usually invited by media organisations wishing to monitor the reception of their products by the audience/consumer.

**feeding frenzy:** a term derived from the practice of fish or predator animals rushing to the smell of blood in order to partake of a kill.
■ When applied to the media, in particular the press, the term describes the intensive coverage of a sensational story, often broken by one newspaper and then followed up by many others. High-profile murder cases, cases that cause public outrage and issues involving the behaviour of celebrities and politicians are the most likely subjects (see **kiss and tell**).
■ *e.g.* Jamie Bulger murder case (1993), Soham murder case (2003) and Sven Goran Eriksson's relationship with television personality Ulrika Jonsson (2003)

**feminism:** political movement to advance the status of women by challenging values, social constructions and socioeconomic practices which disadvantage women and favour men.
■ The movement emerged from the liberation culture of the 1960s, although individual feminists argued for women's rights from a much earlier time.
■ Feminism has provided an important perspective for the critique of media products, especially from the standpoint of **representation**, and has sought to challenge dominant ideologies which reinforce **patriarchal** values.
■ Feminism encompasses various perspectives, e.g. **black feminism, liberal feminism, Marxist feminism, radical feminism** and **post-feminism**.

**femme fatale:** in French *film noir* theory, a female character who uses her sexuality, often in devious, disreputable, secretive ways, to achieve the ends she desires.

■ The *femme fatale* is a dangerous character whose sex appeal often disarms the male protagonist and allows her to manipulate the action.

■ In the 1940s, when sexuality was often associated with moral corruption, the *femme fatale* was at once exciting to an audience and to be condemned for her amoral behaviour.

■ *e.g.* Demi Moore plays a modern *femme fatale* in the film *Disclosure* (Barry Levinson, 1994). Classic *femmes fatales* include Barbara Stanwyck in *Double Indemnity* (Billy Wilder, 1944) and Gloria Grahame in *Human Desire* (Fritz Lang, 1954).

**fifteen-minutes-of-fame:** a phrase associated with pop artist Andy Warhol who said, in the early 1970s, that in a media-dominated world everybody could be famous for 15 minutes.

■ The term can be used to describe the celebrity-from-nobody culture generated by reality television shows such as *Big Brother* and the fame experienced by 'Nasty' Nick Bateman and Jade Goody.

**Film Council:** government-funded organisation responsible for the encouragement and promotion of a successful film industry in the UK.

■ The Film Council provides grants to support new film productions and also supports the British Film Institute.

**Film Distributors Association:** the trade body for film distributors in the UK.

■ Film distribution is part of a multimillion pound business. In the UK alone, it was worth £800 million in box-office takings in 2004.

■ Association members include: Icon, Twentieth Century Fox, Pathé, Buena Vista, Eros, Columbia Tri-Star, Warner Brothers (Time Warner) and Metrodome.

***film noir* (French for 'black film' or 'dark film'):** a term originally coined by French film critics to describe a style of film produced in the USA during the mid to late 1940s.

■ *Film noir* treatments can be identified in many contemporary films (e.g. *Blade Runner*, Ridley Scott, 1982). The term *neo noir* is used to describe films that employ *film noir* plots, characters and iconography in a contemporary setting (e.g. *Se7en*, David Fincher, 1995).

■ *e.g.* *The Big Sleep* (Howard Hawks, 1946)

**film stock:** unexposed film yet to be used in a production.

**final cut:** the edited version of a film, as prepared for cinema release.

■ *TIP* The final cut represents a balance of commercial and artistic interests, therefore control over it is important (see director's cut). Films may often be altered or adapted once preview audience feedback is assessed. If the preview audience prefers a happy to a tragic ending, this alteration is sometimes made at the final stage to help ensure the film's commercial success.

■ Director David Lynch disowned the science-fiction film *Dune* (1984) when it became clear that a variety of commercial interests had interfered with the film's narrative structure and dialogue in a bid to make it more commercially successful.

**Financial Times (FT):** a niche-market British daily financial newspaper owned by **Pearson**. Made distinctive by its pink colour, the *FT* is required reading for its specialist audience of city brokers, financiers, business executives and share dealers. Apart from its extensive coverage of finance and business affairs, it has wide coverage of the arts and world economic and business news.

■ The *FT* is very much a British institution but its future may lie in extending its appeal to a world market.

■ Circulation figures: 422,519 (January 2005).

**fish eye lens:** a camera lens of short focal length with a wide field of vision, usually producing a circular image.

**Five (known as Channel 5 until September 2002):** independent commercial terrestrial television station, launched in 1997 as a result of a requirement in the **Broadcasting Act of 1990** for the **Independent Television Commission (ITC)** to establish a fifth terrestrial channel in the UK.

■ With difficulties involving uninspired programming and poor signal quality in many parts of the UK, the channel had a slow start with low viewing figures. An improvement in programmes increased its share of the terrestrial market.

■ The licence was awarded on the basis of competitive tender with the aim of appealing to a 'modern **mainstream**' audience. Its owners were **Pearson, United News and Media**, CLT Ufa, (a European TV company) and Warburg Pincus and Co. (a US company). In 2000, the German company RTL acquired a 65% stake in Five, leaving United Business Media with 35%.

■ In 2003, Five was awarded a new 10-year licence by the ITC.

■ Five agreed a partnership with **Zip** television, a specialist in interactive advertising, in 2004.

■ *Five News* has gained a reputation for informal presentation and a younger infotainment treatment style, and in 2004 chose Sky News rather than ITN as its news provider.

■ *TIP* Critics argue that Five began the dumbing down of news presentation and content which has since been adopted by other channels.

**Flaherty, Robert J. (1884–1951):** pioneer documentary film maker, famous for *Nanook of the North* (1922).

■ *Nanook of the North* is an account of the daily life of an Inuit tribe living on Hudson's Bay in Canada. The film focuses on the character of Nanook and follows him hunting, building an igloo and generally surviving in harsh conditions. Flaherty lived with the Inuit as he filmed them and staged some of the scenes before organising his footage into a coherent narrative.

■ At that time, documentary films were known as 'travelogues'.

**flashback:** a scene in a film which disrupts the chronological narrative by going backward in time to recall past events.

**Fleet Street:** street in London where the majority of British national newspapers used to be produced and printed; the term was used metonymically to stand for the whole newspaper industry.

■ Newspaper production was largely transferred to Wapping in east London during the 1980s when the industry moved from hot metal processes to computer technology.

**flyer:** leaflet, usually A5 size, used to publicise a service, event, film etc.

■ Flyers are relatively cheap to produce and can be distributed freely to a wide audience, often being handed out in the street. Their effectiveness is limited by lack of specific targeting, with many being wasted or quickly disposed of by recipients.

**fly-on-the-wall:** a documentary production where hidden or discretely placed cameras are allowed unlimited access to the subject at all times and where the subjects' behaviour is assumed not to be influenced by the camera's presence.

**folk culture:** a sentimental and nostalgic golden-age view of the traditional way of life of ordinary, pre-industrial, working-class or peasant communities as constructed by outsiders.

■ Folk culture is seen as free from both the pretensions of high culture and the mediated commercial values of mass culture, and therefore, deriving as it does from people's daily, collective activities, seen as intrinsically more authentic and valuable.

■ *TIP* The merits of folk culture are often only apparent to academic outsiders and not recognised by actual participants in the culture themselves.

**folk devil:** a descriptive term used by sociologist Stan Cohen to describe groups in society which are targeted or demonised by the media as presenting a moral threat and are therefore the focus of moral panic.

■ Folk devils are treated as scapegoats and hate figures whose behaviour is disruptive of mainstream values and ideology.

■ *e.g.* new age travellers, asylum seekers, benefit defrauders

**footprint:** the area of the earth's surface covered by transmissions from a single communications satellite.

**Foucault, Michel (1926–84):** French academic whose work in the fields of sociology, politics, cultural studies and sexuality has been extremely influential.

■ Foucault's investigations of sexual identity and lifestyle, the self and the ways in which power is exercised in society are important in furthering our understanding of how the media influence these debates.

**found image:** an image or photograph from an existing media source which is incorporated into a new media text.

■ Found images, in the form of historical archive footage or celebrity photographs, are used by all media producers, and are always acknowledged in the closing credits for copyright reasons.

■ In his film *Schindler's List* (1993), director Steven Spielberg accessed and viewed large amounts of newsreel footage taken by Nazi cameramen during the Second World War and, to add a sense of documentary accuracy and immediacy to his film, he re-filmed whole sequences on black and white film stock.

■ *TIP* Found images should be used with great caution when constructing media projects as assessment usually includes judging the originality of work. If they are essential for the purpose of the artefact, as with images of pop celebrities or national figures, they should always be acknowledged.

**four Cs:** a term coined in the 1980s by advertising agency Young and Rubicam to explain the changing pattern of consumer behaviour identified during this period.

■ The four Cs or categories of consumer were defined as achievers, aspirers, mainstreamers and reformers. It was argued that these consumer groups sought out and acquired products which reinforced their sense of identity and values.

■ This approach to marketing indicated a growing awareness of the need to target individuals, their lifestyle and identity rather than viewing them as part of a mass market. It also represented a move away from the social classification approach of the ABC1 scale.

**fourth wall:** the imaginary invisible wall through which an audience views film, television and stage drama productions.

■ The fourth wall is broken when a character addresses the audience directly. Most film and theatre productions involve narratives in which audiences are observers looking in as unseen voyeurs of the events put before them. This role is challenged when actors make asides directed at the audience, so involving them more closely with the action.

■ The fourth wall is obviously not present in many television genres where presenters, news readers etc. address the audience directly. This creates the distinctive intimacy and interactive feeling of non-fiction television, which has been further enhanced by new interactive technologies.

**framing:** the process of selecting what is to be framed by a particular film shot, for example, characters, setting and iconography.

■ Across a scene, framing determines how the action is perceived by the audience. It includes such elements as background detail, lighting source and the emphasis given to specific characters within a shot.

■ Framing can determine how the audience perceives character relations in terms of dominance and submission and the weighting given to each character. For example, a foregrounded character can be seen as dominant whereas a character in the background appears less important.

**franchise:** the process by which independent commercial companies are awarded contracts to broadcast under regulation from the appropriate regulatory body.

■ The regulatory body for television was initially the **Independent Broadcasting Authority**, followed by the **Independent Television Commission**, which was replaced by **Ofcom** in 2003.

■ Franchises are licences to broadcast under contractual arrangements for a fixed period, and the successful bidder must demonstrate suitability in terms of financial viability and commitment to programme quality within the terms of the contract.

**Frankfurt School:** a group of German **Marxist** intellectuals who began developing their critical theory in the 1920s but who were forced to leave Nazi Germany in the 1930s to continue their work in the USA.

■ The principal members of the school are Max Horkheimer (philosophy and social psychology), Theodor Adorno (sociology and philosophy), Herbert Marcuse (politics and philosophy), Eric Fromm (psychoanalysis and social psychology) and Walter Benjamin (sociology of literature and art).

■ The Frankfurt School is important for its study of what it called 'the **culture industry**', which it saw as performing a highly manipulative role in advanced capitalist societies, containing and subverting opposition on behalf of the ruling **elite** and **dominant ideology**.

**freesheet:** a local weekly or monthly newspaper, distributed free of charge, either at home or on the street.

■ With a wide local distribution and costs covered by advertising, freesheets represent a considerable challenge to the traditional purchased local newspaper. Although readers have not made a decision to buy a paper, they are still likely to read a freesheet delivered to their door, thereby guaranteeing exposure to the advertising. With so many freesheets available, readers are less likely to purchase a traditional newspaper.

■ Many traditional local newspapers now provide a freesheet version of their publication.

■ *e.g.* the *Metro* range of publications owned by **Associated Newspapers**

**freeview:** free digital television service, a successor to onDigital/itvDigital, launched in October 2002 and obtained via a digital set top box.

■ Freeview offers 30-channel television and is an inducement for viewers to 'go digital', in line with government policy to digitalise the whole country by 2012.

**French New Wave:** a style of filming developed in France (1958–68) and associated with the work of directors Jean-Luc Godard, Claude Chabrol, Eric Rohmer, Jacques Rivette and Francois Truffaut.

■ New Wave films were influenced by the writings of film critic Andre Bazin in the journal *Cahiers du Cinéma*. They are characterised by their 'realism', naturalistic *mise en scène* and use of deep focus.

■ *e.g.* Classic examples include *Les Quatre Cents Coups* (*The Four Hundred Blows*) (François Truffaut, 1959) and *À bout de souffle* (*Breathless*) (Jean-Luc Godard, 1960).

**gaffer:** the member of a film production crew who acts as chief technician, particularly in relation to lighting.

**Galtung, Johan and Ruge, Marie:** Norwegian researchers responsible for devising a set of news values (1965), which describes the circumstances and conditions required for events to become news.

**game show:** television genre usually involving members of the public or a studio audience competing in a game to win prizes.
- In spite of apparently generous prizes and cash payouts, game shows are essentially cheap television presented in front of an audience, without high production costs, and with sponsorship and advertising usually producing a healthy profit.

**gangster:** describes a film genre based around the activities of a criminal gang or gangs.
- The first film identified as 'gangster' was *The Musketeers of Pig Alley* (D. W. Griffith, 1912) which created a rationale for the genre based on New York tenement life, with themes of poverty, crime and retribution. *Regeneration* (Raoul Walsh, 1915), also set in New York, told the story of the rise to gangster status of an Irish/US immigrant from the slums.
- Gangster movies represent the myth of America, where the conflict between good and evil is played out in the slums of big cities. The aspirational dreams of gangsters relate to the lives of poor, city-dwelling cinema-goers faced with the challenge between the legitimate desire to achieve the American Dream and the illegitimate use of crime as the means to pursue that goal. Gangster films are therefore usually morally ambivalent.
- Concerns about the positive representation of gangsters as 'folk' or 'tragic heroes' troubled the Hays Office, and after 1934 studios were forced to insert moral pronouncements condemning the behaviour of the gangsters featured in films. However, gangsters remain folk heroes, particularly within the family saga tradition, e.g. the 'supportive ' Italian/US extended family of the *Godfather* trilogy (Francis Ford Coppola, 1971–1990).

g

- The gangster genre is adaptable and transfers to any city and cultural environment where rival gangs struggle for mastery or escape, often against a background of oppression and poverty, e.g. *City of God* (Fernando Meirelles, 2002) set in Rio de Janeiro.
- *e.g.* Landmarks in gangster movies: *Underworld* (Josef von Sternberg, 1927), *City Streets* (Rouben Mamoulian, 1931), *Little Caesar* (Mervyn Le Roy, 1931), *The Public Enemy* (William Wellman, 1931), *Scarface* (Howard Hawks, 1932 — remade in 1983 by Brian De Palma), *Bonnie and Clyde* (Arthur Penn, 1967), *Goodfellas* (Martin Scorsese, 1990), *Reservoir Dogs* (Quentin Tarantino, 1992), *Casino* (Martin Scorsese, 1995) and *Gangs of New York* (Martin Scorsese, 2003).
- *e.g.* British variants: the black comedy *Lock, Stock and Two Smoking Barrels* (Guy Ritchie, 1998), *Snatch* (Guy Ritchie, 2000) and the psychodrama variant *Sexy Beast* (Jonathan Glazer, 2001).
- *TIP* Famous quotations reflect the genre's values: 'As far back as I can remember, I always wanted to be a gangster', opening line of *Goodfellas* (Martin Scorsese, 1990); 'I believe in America', opening line of *The Godfather* (Francis Ford Coppola, 1971).

**gangster rap:** a style of rap music in which the lyrics seem to glorify violent and aggressive acts.
- It has been accused of influencing the behaviour of young people, particularly black people, and has been the focus of **moral panic** concerning increases in violence and gun crime.

**gatefold:** a multipage, large-format, foldout newspaper advertisement printed on heavy paper.

**gatekeeper:** a person in a position to pass, block or alter a media message, for example an **editor**.
- By selecting some stories and rejecting others, gatekeepers are said to have the power to set **agendas** and so influence public opinion.
- **Pluralist** critics argue that the decisions of news editors are taken solely on the judgement of whether or not a story satisfies **news values** criteria **Marxists** would argue that the decisions tend to benefit the agenda set by **dominant ideology** and so serve the interests of **capitalism**.

**gender:** psychological and cultural aspects of behaviour associated with masculinity and femininity, acquired through socialisation, in accordance with the expectations of a particular society.
- **Representations** of gender increasingly challenge traditional concepts of masculinity and femininity.
- Girl power, launched as a marketing device for the *Spice Girls* in the early 1990s, created new role models of assertive young women, rejecting the traditional passive female role.

g

■ Traditional masculine traits of violent aggression, sexual promiscuity and high levels of alcohol consumption are increasingly represented without gender distinction, and female representations in film may challenge or subvert traditional femininity and female roles, e.g. *Kill Bill: Vol. 1* and *Kill Bill: Vol. 2* (Quentin Tarantino, 2003, 2004) and *Tomb Raider* (Simon West, 2001).

■ Masculinity is represented increasingly as soft or ambivalent. Men can now cry, show affection for babies and talk about their feelings openly, all characteristics traditionally associated with femininity. Males are also shown as uncertain about their gender identity, e.g. *Fight Club* (David Fincher, 1999).

**gendered consumption:** the way that gender affects our consumption of media texts.

■ Ann Gray suggested (1992) that women prefer open-ended narratives, such as soap operas, whereas men preferred closed narratives with a clear resolution, for example, police dramas. The concept of 'women's fiction' (Christine Geraghty, 1991) involves identifying characteristics in media texts that appeal to women.

■ *e.g.* Soap operas attracting large female audiences have strong female leads, deal with personal relationships in the domestic sphere and contain an element of escapism.

**genre:** key concept a category of media products classed as being similar in form and type.

■ Film, magazine, newspaper and television are all media genres. Types of film, magazine, newspaper and television programme are also genres. Westerns and musicals are film genres, lifestyle magazines are a magazine genre, tabloids and broadsheets are newspaper genres, situation comedies, crime dramas and soap operas are television genres.

■ Genres operate alongside **narrative** constructions in line with audience expectations, for example, magazines of a particular genre are expected to contain a specific kind of narrative **discourse**.

■ Genres can be further divided into **subgenres**.

**genre theory:** an explanation of the role played by genre in differentiating media texts and aligning **audiences**.

■ Genre theorists consider the relationship between audiences, media texts and media producers and the ways in which genres, particularly in film, can be used by producers to target specific audience groups, with predictable expectations of audience numbers and responses.

■ *e.g.* In explaining their appeal to audiences, Richard Dyer (1973) argues that genres are pleasurable because they offer escapist fantasies into fictional worlds which remove the boredom and pressures of reality. He sees these worlds as

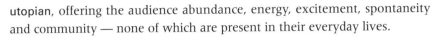

utopian, offering the audience abundance, energy, excitement, spontaneity and community — none of which are present in their everyday lives.

**Gerbner, George (1919–):** US media researcher who in 1956 produced a general process model of mass communication on the following lines:

> *someone; perceives an event; and reacts; in a situation; through some means; to make available materials; in some form; and context; conveying content; with some consequence*

■ Gerbners's model breaks down the communication process in such a way as to identify all the component stages and activities. Gerbner emphasises the variable nature of the perception of an event by an individual and the way in which a message is perceived by the receiver.

■ *TIP* Unlike semiotic approaches to the creation of media texts and their reception, Gerbner does not address how meaning is created.

**Giddens, Anthony (1938–):** sociologist and director (2005) of the London School of Economics. Giddens is an important theorist in the field of 'late modernity', the democratisation of all aspects of life, together with globalisation and the changing role of the state.

■ Giddens's approach focuses on how we construct our identity, which is no longer given to us through socialisation and inheritance. We constantly work on our 'self' and seek to express who we are through the adoption of lifestyles often represented in the media. These representations play an important part in helping us structure and review our identity and help us to make personal decisions about ourselves, our relationships and the world around us.

**Glasgow University Media Group:** media research group established in 1974 under the leadership of Greg Philo, following the group's production of a book, *Bad News* (1974).

■ The group focuses on conducting media research in the empiricist tradition, relying on extensive data from interviews, case studies and content analysis to form their conclusions.

■ Working in a Marxist tradition, the group's principal concerns are with the ways in which power structures and processes shape media content, tastes and style. They are interested in how actual events are represented in news, rather than in theoretical positioning.

■ They insist on the essential difference between image and reality and are critical of theorists such as Jean Baudrillard who make broad pronouncements on issues, for example, the merging of image and reality through simulacra, without providing any empirical evidence. Members of the group see themselves as closer to journalists than to many academics.

■ *TIP* Recent work by the group, *Bad News from Israel* (2004), focuses on the Israeli/Palestinian conflict.

**g**

**globalisation:** the growing tendency of industrial and commercial companies to merge and operate on an international rather than a national or regional basis.

**global village:** term coined by Marshall McLuhan to describe the shrinking effect that mass communication has had on the world.
- Now that the electronic media can flash news around the world in an instant, distances are no longer significant and the world has become like a village in which everybody seems to know everyone else's business.

**GMG:** see Guardian Media Group.

**golden age:** an ideal period in human history which is looked back on with nostalgia.
- In film history, the golden age of Hollywood refers to the studio system in place between 1930 and 1948, when films were produced on a production-line basis around celebrity film stars, whose careers were dependent on their studio contracts.

**gothic:** describes a film treatment style associated with horror films.
- Two influential novels, Mary Shelley's *Frankenstein* (1818) and Bram Stoker's *Dracula* (1897), provide the iconography for gothic horror: ruined castles, graveyards, dark and gloomy settings, bats, wolves and wild and threatening natural environments.
- *TIP* Gothic treatments exist in films other than the horror genre, for example *Batman* (Tim Burton, 1989) and *Edward Scissorhands* (Tim Burton, 1990).

**Gramsci, Antonio (1871–1937):** leader of the Italian communist party, imprisoned by Benito Mussolini from 1926 until his death in 1937.
- Gramsci's writings in his 'Prison Notebooks' (1930s) were an important source for the development of theories of ideology and the role of the media in reproducing dominant ideology.
- Gramsci used the term hegemony to describe the way in which the dominant elite can maintain its power over the economic, political and cultural direction of a society. The values that sustain elites in power are reproduced every day by the media and made to seem like the common sense views of the majority, so that any challenge to them is marginalised.

**Granada:** former Independent Television (ITV) news company, with a strong tradition of regional programming in the north and northwest of England, which merged with Carlton in 2003 to form a single commercial television company called ITV plc.
- Granada proved to be among the most successful and enduring of the original ITV companies and grew to be one of the largest broadcasting and media

organisations in the UK. The increasing tendency toward larger media organisations with global reach led to its merger with Carlton in 2003.

**graveyard slot:** another term for late-night Sunday television, a slot in which schedulers bury dead programmes or where they send failing programmes to die.

■ Sunday late-night viewing figures are low.

**grey market:** advertising and marketing term for the over 50s and the retired, who are increasingly seen as a lucrative market for specific goods and services and are consequently targeted by advertisers and the media.

■ The over 50s are currently 20 million strong and increasing. They hold 80% of the nation's wealth and show an increasing tendency to spend their money on holidays and leisure activities, rather than leaving it to their children.

■ However, predictions about the value of the grey market and the amount of wealth available to the over 50s, are subject to changes in lifestyle. The traditional family pattern is the norm in only 30% of households, with the young more likely to return home after college, so imposing new financial burdens on parents. Men in their 50s can experience divorce, remarriage and the starting of new families, with consequent financial commitments.

■ Traditional grey market areas include: holidays, gardening, leisure and antiques magazines and second homes. However, with life seemingly becoming more cyclical and less linear, stereotypes of the over 50s can be misleading.

**Grierson, John (1898–1972):** film maker, often called 'the father of documentary' and credited with both inventing the term and making the first of the genre, *Drifters* (1929).

■ His best known work is probably *Night Mail* (1936), which he produced about the post office mail train, made famous by the poem of the same name by W. H. Auden.

■ Influenced by the work of Walter Lippmann, Grierson saw documentary as a means of shaping public opinion.

**grip:** individual on a film set responsible for moving and arranging scenery, lighting cameras and other equipment.

***Guardian:*** the principal left-of-centre quality national daily newspaper, with a circulation of 376,000 copies (January 2005).

■ Part of the Guardian Media Group and owned by the Scott Trust, the *Guardian* has a firm position on the left of the British cultural and political scene.

**Guardian Media Group (GMG):** a media organisation overseen by the Scott Trust which owns the *Guardian*, the *Observer* and the *Manchester Evening*

*News* newspapers, together with other print publications and radio and digital television companies.

**gutter:** a section of the pages of a magazine where the centre division, usually carrying the binding staples or glue, takes up a vertical strip of the printed pages on either side.

■ The 'gutter' means that a full page is not fully legible and that allowance has to be made when lining up pages to ensure that part of the copy and any images used are not lost to view.

**gutter press:** a term used to describe the tabloid press, derived from its tendency to build stories around the worst aspects of human behaviour, e.g. sexual infidelity or misconduct, betrayal, impropriety, corruption and homicide.

**Hachette:** the largest French magazine-publishing company, owner of *Marie Claire*, formerly partnered with Emap in the publishing of *Elle*.

**Hall, Stuart (1932–):** a leading academic figure in the development of media and cultural studies theory, former head of the Centre for Contemporary Cultural Studies and now an Open University professor.

- Hall is responsible for highlighting the ideological effects of media content and in particular the way in which dominant ideology is reinforced.
- His 1970s' studies of the representation of race on British television have been the basis for a continuing debate on positive, negative or non-existent representations.
- Hall's approach belongs to the Marxist tradition and follows the work of Antonio Gramsci in explaining how continuous exposure to mainstream media content can have lasting effects by reinforcing common sense or hegemonic attitudes, beliefs and values.
- He also focuses on degrees of audience resistance to media content and intended closure, exploring the possibility of individuals adopting dominant, negotiated or oppositional readings of a polysemic media text. Hall proposed an encoding/decoding model where the meaning of a text is framed by the producer and decoded by readers in line with their own background and circumstances.
- *TIP* Hall's approach can be criticised for relying too heavily on possible variations in readings of media texts and not enough on empirical research directed at the power structures which determine the content of those texts in the first place.

**Hammer Studios:** British film studio famous for the production of horror films in the gothic and vampire subgenres during the 1950s and 1970s.

- With films featuring the stars Vincent Price, Christopher Lee and Peter Cushing, Hammer developed a particular gothic-fantasy style which seems tame and unconvincing to today's horror audience.

■ *e.g.* *The Curse of Frankenstein* (Terence Fisher, 1957), *Dracula* (Terence Fisher, 1958)

**hammocking:** the practice of television schedulers placing an unpopular programme between two popular programmes to attract viewers to the less popular offering.

■ Hammocking reflects Reithian values of the 'public service' obligation to 'educate' viewers and listeners. The idea that you could use popular programming to draw the public to more worthwhile, challenging output (e.g. a classical concert, a philosophical debate or a Shakespeare play) worked when listeners and viewers had little else to choose from.

■ *e.g.* A large audience can be brought to an *Omnibus* arts documentary by placing it after a hit comedy such as *The Royle Family* and before a popular entertainment programme such as *They Think It's All Over*.

■ *TIP* With increased viewer choice, hammocking is less effective since viewers will switch channels when they realise that a given programme does not meet their mood or expectations.

**hand-held camera:** a portable camera.

■ Any domestic video camera is 'hand held' in principle and the results of the filming are often wobbly and amateurish. Hand-held cameras are used professionally to create naturalistic, realist and point-of-view effects in films and to convey an impression of everyday life rather than mediated experience.

■ *e.g.* *The Blair Witch Project* (Daniel Myrick, 1999) was constructed from the raw hand-held footage taken by the protagonists as a video diary of their frightening experiences.

**hard news:** news involving political, economic, social and environmental events of significant national and international importance.

■ Hard news usually requires audiences to have some background knowledge and a willingness to concentrate on detail in order to be fully understood. With the tendency toward dumbing down, hard news is frequently either diluted or replaced by soft news with more human-interest content.

**Hays Office:** another name for The Motion Picture Producers and Distributors of America, a self-regulating body set up under the chairmanship of William H. Hays in 1922 to improve the image of the film industry.

■ In 1930 it produced a production code (also known as the Hays Code) of cinematic practice, listing all subjects forbidden. The code was essentially a system of strict censorship which acted as a constraint on film makers. It lasted until 1967 when it was declared unconstitutional and was replaced by a ratings system.

■ The Hays Code prohibited the representation of revenge in a modern setting, sex scenes were banned altogether and film makers were not even allowed to show a man and a woman sitting on a bed together. Scenes of violence were strictly censored and it was forbidden to show a gun being fired and a bullet hitting a person in the same shot.

**H certificate:** film classification introduced by the **British Board of Film Censors** in 1932 following the development of the vampire horror movie *Dracula* (Tod Browning, 1931), and *Frankenstein* (James Whale, 1931).
- The certificate identified a horror film as being suitable for those over 16 only. It was merged with the new X certificate in 1951.

**head-on shot:** a type of shot in which the action comes directly toward the camera.
- Head-on shots are often used in war or action movies to enhance the sense of involvement and excitement of the audience, for example, charging cavalry may be directed at the camera.
- *e.g.* *Waterloo* (Sergei Bondachuk, 1970)

**hegemonic reading:** see dominant reading.

**hegemony:** the total cultural, economic and political dominance achieved by the ruling **elite** in a society.
- The term was first developed by Antonio **Gramsci**.
- Once a particular group has achieved hegemony, their viewpoint becomes accepted by public opinion as **common sense**, making it difficult for opposition groups to make an effective challenge.
- *e.g.* From 1979–97, the Conservative Party achieved hegemony with its policies for transforming the economy. Margaret Thatcher's phrase 'there is no alternative' expressed common sense views widely held at the time.

***Hello!:*** UK celebrity magazine originating in Spain as *¡Hola!*, with articles on celebrities, royalty and the world of entertainment.
- *Hello!* faces strong competition from its rival *OK!*.

**heritage film:** a film based on a classic piece of literature or on historical events.
- Heritage films are characterised by meticulous attention to period detail and settings. Often associated with British cinema, they are well received in the world market, particularly in the USA. They are criticised by some as representing the past in an idealised and stereotypical way.
- *e.g.* works by directors Ismail Merchant and James Ivory such as *A Room with a View* (1986), *Howard's End* (1992) and *Remains of the Day* (1993)

**hero:** the principal male or female **protagonist** in any narrative, with whom the audience identifies and who exhibits moral virtues in line with **dominant ideology**.

**hidden agenda:** a journalistic term applied to politicians, organisations and individuals who profess one set of priorities in public while concealing another set of priorities that is representative of their true motives and intentions.

■ *e.g.* Governments seeking re-election will campaign on the basis of their successes and future plans for improvements in services, while seeking to avoid discussing tax rises which they may intend to introduce after being re-elected.

**highbrow:** a term used to describe media texts with a demanding intellectual content and requiring specialist knowledge in order to be understood.

■ Highbrow texts are often considered **elitist** because they are accessible only to those with the privilege of a particular background or education (see **lowbrow, popular culture, dumbing down**).

**high concept film:** a film with a big budget and state-of-the-art special effects, usually associated with US productions.

■ *e.g. The Matrix* (Wachowski Brothers, 1999), which introduced the special effect called bullet-time.

**high culture:** see highbrow.

**Hollywood:** a district of Los Angeles, California, the centre of the US film industry during the **golden age** of the studio system, 1930–48.

■ The **globalisation** of media industries has meant that films can be made anywhere in the world, so that the location of Hollywood has become less important in terms of actual film production. Major film studios still have their corporate headquarters there and it is a major centre of corporate activity and film finance.

■ Hollywood remains a playground for the super rich and their glamorous, celebrity lifestyles.

**homage:** when one film director pays tribute to another by including images, scenes or stylistic features typical of the other director as an acknowledgement of his/her influence and importance.

■ In *What Lies Beneath* (Robert Zemeckis, 2000), the director is deliberately copying plot devices, techniques and scenes used by Alfred Hitchcock in films such as *Rear Window* (1954) and *Psycho* (1960).

**Homechoice:** a combined broadband **internet** and **digital** television service, operating via a British Telecom line, using a decoder box, and currently offering 1,000 movies, 80-channel digital television, 3,000 music videos, numerous television series and broadband internet.

■ An example of technological **convergence**, Homechoice is currently only available in some areas of the UK.

**horizontal integration:** the merger of competing companies from the same line of business and involved at the same level of activity.

■ Mergers or take-overs that would allow particular companies to dominate a market and create a **monopoly** are subject to laws restricting ownership and government regulation.

■ *e.g.* the merger of **Carlton** and **Granada** to form **ITV plc**

**horror:** describes a film **genre** which aims to frighten the audience.

■ Horror film narratives work on basic human fears: of the dark, of the alien and unknown, of death and the supernatural, of being alone, of other people, of insanity, of extreme violence, of sexual abuse. Settings can be in alien environments or in the everyday surroundings of the characters.

■ Since the first horror film, *Nosferatu* (F. W. Murnau, 1922), horror has been an established genre and has varied and adapted in a range of **subgenres** to reflect changing contexts and the concerns and fears of different generations. *Psycho* (Alfred Hitchcock, 1960) was the first film to make the source of the horror a psychologically disturbed individual — the boy next door rather than a monster.

■ Subgenres of horror have their own specific narrative patterns and **iconography** and include psychotic individuals, gothic and vampire tales, demons, the possessed and the spirit world, the taking over of the body by aliens, zombies, and alien monsters (see **gothic, vampire movie, zombie movie, science fiction**).

■ *e.g.* Classic horror films and genre variants include: *Phantom of the Opera* (Rupert Julian, 1925), *Dr Jekyll and Mr Hyde* (Rouben Mamoulian, 1931), *Dracula* (Tod Browning, 1931), *Frankenstein* (James Whale, 1931), *The Mummy* (Karl Freund, 1932), *Invasion of the Body Snatchers* (Don Siegel, 1956), *Whatever Happened to Baby Jane?* (Robert Aldrich, 1962), *Repulsion* (Roman Polanski, 1965), *Night of the Living Dead* (George Romero, 1968), *Rosemary's Baby* (Roman Polanski, 1968), *The Texas Chainsaw Massacre* (Tobe Hooper, 1972), *The Exorcist* (William Friedkin, 1973), *Jaws* (Steven Spielberg, 1975), *Carrie* (Brian De Palma, 1976), *The Omen* (Tobe Hooper, 1976), *Halloween* (John Carpenter, 1978), *The Shining* (Stanley Kubrick, 1980), *Poltergeist* (Tobe Hooper, 1982), *A Nightmare on Elm Street* (Wes Craven, 1984), *The Fly* (David Cronenberg, 1986), *Cape Fear* (remake) (Martin Scorsese, 1991), *The Silence of the Lambs* (Jonathan Demme, 1991), *Scream* (Wes Craven, 1996), *Ring* (Hideo Nakata, 1998), *The Blair Witch Project* (Daniel Myrick, 1999).

**hospital drama:** a television genre centred around hospitals and the lives of hospital staff and patients.

■ Hospitals have always been a popular setting for television drama and romance, the first British series being ATV's *Emergency Ward Ten* (1957–67).

■ *e.g.* US *ER*, UK *Casualty* and spin-off *Holby City*

■ *TIP* Since the operation of the National Health Service is a sensitive subject politically, hospital dramas often contain a strong **social action** element where funding issues, management styles, shortages, malpractices and a range of other political, social and economic concerns relating to hospitals and the medical profession are highlighted, both for their entertainment value and also as a means of encouraging public debate.

**hot metal process:** the newspaper printing process, now obsolete, which involved the casting of hot metal type in full lines by a Linotype machine.

■ The method was replaced by computerisation during the 1980s.

**HTTP:** see Hypertext Transfer Protocol.

**human interest:** descriptive term for news stories that revolve around people's everyday problems and experience, feelings and emotions.

■ A human-interest **angle** on a disaster like 9/11 would concentrate on individual personal accounts of survival, loss, feelings, hopes, fears and other emotions.

**hybrid:** a cross between one film genre and another.

■ *e.g.* *From Dusk till Dawn* (Robert Rodriguez, 1996) starts as a crime drama and becomes a **vampire movie**.

■ *TIP* Hybrids are becoming ever more popular since they allow film makers to increase their potential audience by including elements that appeal to more than one group. *Titanic* (James Cameron, 1997) is a cross between historical reconstruction, disaster, romance and thriller and as such appeals to all ages and both genders.

**hype:** the generation by the media of excitement over an issue or product through intense and often exaggerated coverage.

■ The intense publicity surrounding a product launch can involve hype to secure maximum public interest. Hype may also be used to raise expectations, often unrealistically.

■ *e.g.* British athlete Paula Radcliffe was subject to hyped media expectation over her expected performance in the Athens Olympics in 2004. Her subsequent failure led to national disappointment and negative media coverage. The expected performance of the England football team is always subject to hype and inflated expectation, with consequent pressure on players and often great national disappointment with results.

**hyperreality:** a heightened and artificial sense of reality created by simulated environments, such as theme parks and **cyberculture**.

**hypertext transfer protocol (HTTP):** the set of rules or language used for transferring and exchanging files (images, graphics text, sound and video) on the internet.

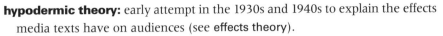

**hypodermic theory:** early attempt in the 1930s and 1940s to explain the effects media texts have on audiences (see effects theory).

■ Based on the assumed 'passive' nature of a mass audience, the theory argues that consumption of media texts is like the injection of a drug and that the audiences' behaviour and opinions are therefore directly affected.

■ *TIP* The theory, although useful in its time, in particular in relation to the mass propaganda machines of Nazi Germany and Stalinist Russia, is now considered to be an oversimplification of complex processes.

**hypothesis:** a theory or supposition of the possible pattern of causes and effects, within given social and cultural structures, to be tested by research.

■ A hypothesis forms the basis of many independent study assignments.

■ *e.g.* Contemporary representations of women in film as self-motivated individuals and the equals of men challenge the assumptions of Mulvey's 'male gaze' theory — an assessment of female leads in *The Matrix* (Wachowski Brothers, 1999) and *Kill Bill: Vols 1 and 2* (Quentin Tarantino, 2003–04).

■ *TIP* When forming a hypothesis, you should always ensure that a clear proposition is related to known research criteria, with clearly defined texts to be examined.

**IBA:** see Independent Broadcasting Authority.

**icon:** a sign resembling the thing it represents.

■ An icon can also be an image representative of an ideology or religion. Icons were originally religious paintings of Christ and the Virgin Mary and treated as sacred objects.

■ *e.g.* a photograph

■ *TIP* A public figure who, having achieved the ultimate in a particular field, has become the focus of mass adoration is also called an icon, e.g. pop icons such as Kylie Minogue or Madonna.

**iconography:** the distinguishing elements, in terms of props and visual details, which characterise a genre.

■ Genres are said to be recognisable through their characteristic iconography.

■ *e.g.* The iconography of gangster films includes smart suits, guns and fast cars, while Westerns have horses, desert locations, clapboard houses and men in hats.

**ident (short for identity):** the brand image of a media product or service.

■ With a news programme, for example, Channel 4 News, the opening titles, including the logo, and the signature tune or jingle are its ident. Changes in the ident are termed a 'makeover'.

**ideological state apparatus:** term devised by Louis Althusser to describe institutions which are established and controlled by the state and which have the power to reinforce and reproduce dominant ideology.

■ *e.g.* the education system

**ideology:** *key concept* a set of attitudes, beliefs and values held in common by a group of people and culturally reproduced within that community to sustain its particular way of life.

■ Ideologies can be described as dominant, subservient, or oppositional depending on their status within a society (see dominant ideology).

■ *e.g.* capitalism, communism, Christianity and Islam

■ *TIP* Ideology is present in all media texts. You can explore it by assessing the attitudes, beliefs and values within the text and the assumptions made about what the viewer or reader thinks and feels.

**IMAX:** a film production and projection system which combines the use of a huge screen, giant projectors showing 70mm film and digital surround sound to provide the viewer with a unique sense of scale, space and total involvement in the visual and audio experience.

■ IMAX productions are specially commissioned and usually involve outer-space, under-the-sea or other dramatic locations.

■ They are expensive to operate, not widely available and more a showcase for technology than a reflection of everyday viewing opportunities.

**iMovie:** a range of Apple Macintosh audiovisual editing software.

■ iMovie and the more recent iMovie HD for high definition video provide alternatives to the more commonly used Adobe premiere, with many of the user-friendly features that fans of Apple Macintosh computers find attractive.

**in-camera-editing:** a technique of filming shots in the sequence required for the final production so avoiding the need for postproduction editing.

■ *TIP* This is an amateurish, reasonably effective but crude method of film making, which requires careful planning and leaves no room for mistakes. Editing techniques are limited to cuts and fades and the soundtrack usually needs to be added unless diegetic sound, recorded on the film, is all that is required.

***Independent:*** quality daily newspaper, owned, with its sister paper the *Independent on Sunday*, by Independent News and Media.

■ The *Independent*, with a circulation of 257,000 (January 2005), has the lowest circulation of any of the quality newspapers. However, its pioneering of the compact size, its criticism of the 2003 Iraq War and its strongly non-partisan positioning in the political centre have built up a loyal and growing readership.

■ The *Independent on Sunday* (circulation 206,000 January 2005) has established itself as an alternative to the left-of-centre *Observer* for readers seeking a non-partisan and liberal news agenda.

**Independent Broadcasting Authority (IBA):** body established in 1972 to oversee and regulate commercial broadcasting in Britain, replacing the ITA (Independent Television Authority, 1954–72). It was replaced by the Independent Television Commission in 1990.

**independent (indi) producer:** a producer operating outside the structure of large media corporations and usually focusing on products that reflect minority interests.

- Independent films are made without the support of major studios and on a restricted budget.
- The survival and success of independents is important if the variety and range of media texts are to be maintained in a world increasingly dominated by a few giant producers. Many productions involve a co-financing arrangement between different funding agencies.
- *e.g.* *Breaking the Waves* (Lars von Trier, 1996, Denmark/France/Netherlands co-production)

**Independent News and Media:** newspaper publishing company, owner of the *Independent* and *Independent on Sunday*.

**Independent on Sunday:** see *Independent*.

**Independent Television (ITV):** the commercial network of television companies franchised to provide regional independent television coverage from its founding in 1955.

- In spite of its commercial nature, ITV was constrained by a public service requirement, monitored by the Independent Broadcasting Authority (IBA), to ensure that its programmes contained agreed percentages of news, current affairs and quality drama-based productions, together with programmes produced in the UK. Criticism of ITV programme content by the Pilkington Committee (1962) lead to a second channel (BBC 2) being granted to the BBC and not ITV.
- In 1968, major changes in the franchises created five big ITV companies, Thames, London Weekend, Yorkshire, Granada and ATV. Again, after the 1980 franchise review, new companies such as Meridian emerged.
- The progress of deregulation, begun in the 1990s, created further upheavals and changes of franchise and by 2000 Carlton, Granada, United MAI and the Scottish Media Group (together with a few independent franchises) dominated the network, with ITV 1 in England and Wales being controlled entirely by Carlton and Granada. The overall tendency was towards merger, with a few large companies taking control and a consequent reduction in distinctive regional identity. The merger of Carlton and Granada in 2003 created one giant new company, ITV plc formed in February 2004. The company owns 40% of Independent Television News (ITN) and the franchises for the following Channel 3 licences: Anglia, Border, Carlton London, Central Television, HTV, Granada Television, London Weekend, Meridian Broadcasting, Tyne Tees TV, Westcountry and Yorkshire Television together with ITV 2 and 3 and the ITV News Channel.

**Independent Television Commission (ITC):** public body which replaced the Independent Broadcasting Association after deregulation in 1990 and was responsible for monitoring the content and management of independent broadcasting in the UK until 2003, when it was replaced by Ofcom.

**Independent Television News (ITN):** company with responsibility for providing news services to the commercial television sector made up of ITV, Channel 4, the ITV news channel and a further 260 commercial radio stations through Independent Radio News (IRN).

- The ITN news archive is the biggest in the world.
- ITN was founded in 1955 as an independent organisation under the ownership of the then 15 ITV companies. It is now owned by four companies: ITV plc (40%), the *Daily Mail* and General Trust (20%), United Business Media (20%) and Reuters (20%).
- In 2005, ITN lost its contract to supply news to Five (formerly Channel 5) to Sky News.

**infotainment:** the practice of mixing news with entertainment, thereby 'dumbing down' hard news content in order to make news and current affairs programmes more entertaining and of greater appeal to a wider audience.

**innoculation:** the process whereby constant exposure to harrowing media images of war, famine disaster etc. has a numbing and desensitising effect on the viewer.

- Although shocking at first, these images can seem more acceptable and reaction to them can become dulled the more audiences are exposed to them. In this sense, audiences are 'innoculated' against the highly charged emotional content of the images.

**insert:** any advertisement or promotional material produced by advertisers for inclusion in a magazine or newspaper as a separate item.

- An insert may be inserted loose or bound into a publication.

**institution:** *key concept* any of the organisations responsible for the production, marketing, distribution or regulation of media texts.

- Institutions are business and social structures that produce media texts and regulate and structure media activities. They are collectives within which individuals are encouraged to work toward a common goal and to develop working practices based on assumptions about the aims and ethos of the institution. Institutions assume the shared values of all employees and have a status and power relationship with other institutions and the wider public.
- *e.g.* British Broadcasting Corporation, British Sky Broadcasting, Cable News Network, British Board of Film Classification and Ogilvy and Mather

**interactive:** a computer or telecommunication system where the user can have some control over software and is not just a passive recipient.

- *e.g.* a computer game

**interactive media:** media systems which allow two-way communication between individuals and organisations or broadcasters.

■ *e.g.* shopping and banking on the internet, voting in *Pop Idol*

**internet:** the global computer network.

■ The internet is a network that links computers around the world and allows those connected to visit the World Wide Web (www), use e-mail, upload or download files using file transfer protocol (FTP), chat in chat rooms with other users via internet relay chat (IRC) and use telnet to issue commands to distant computers.

■ Since the advent of the World Wide Web in the early 1990s, the internet has dramatically affected communication and the transfer of information and it raises many issues including privacy and security. Computers on the internet communicate by means of an internet protocol address (IP address), similar to a phone number. Inadequately protected computers can be exploited for commercial or criminal purposes by hackers using an IP address to identify a machine.

■ Other problems include the distribution and ready availability of pornography and of copyrighted music, films etc., which major organisations, such as Microsoft, are taking steps to curb.

**internet service provider (ISP):** any company responsible for providing access to the internet via a telephone link.

■ *e.g.* Wanadoo, Onetel

**interpellation:** the process whereby individuals' responses to media texts can be cued by repeating familiar forms.

■ The term was originally used by French Marxist sociologist Louis Althusser.

■ *e.g.* The signature tune and opening titles of soap operas attract an audience's attention and create a receptive state of mind, preparing the audience for what is to follow. The same applies to news programmes, which often have dramatic opening themes, using trumpets and loud chords to draw attention to the importance of news. The medieval town crier's bell would have had the same effect.

**intertextuality:** the practice of deliberately including references to one text in the narrative of another, either as homage to the text referred to or as a device intended to engage the interest of the audience by appealing to their prior knowledge and experience of media texts.

■ Intertextuality can generate levels of meaning for the viewer and anchors a current text within texts of similar or related genre.

■ *e.g.* *Kill Bill: Vol. 1* (Quentin Tarantino, 2003) makes many references to Westerns, gangster and Japanese Samurai films.

**invisible editing:** a moving image editing technique designed to ensure edits follow events in the narrative sequence as unobtrusively as possible.

■ The technique adds to the sense of realism in a film and allows character and narrative to dominate at the expense of auteurist film craft.

**IPC Media:** Britain's largest magazine publisher, with over 100 titles and 22% of the market, selling 350 million magazines a year. IPC Media was taken over by Time Warner in 2001.

■ Titles include *NME, Loaded, Nuts* and *Marie Claire* (on licence, since the title is owned by the French company Hachette)

■ *Marie Claire* is the leading competition to *Cosmopolitan*, and *Nuts* is competing with Emap's *Zoo Weekly* to become top-selling men's weekly.

**iris:** the adjustable circular lens opening which is used to regulate the amount of light entering a camera and reaching the film.

**iris fade (also known as 'iris wipe'):** an editing technique in which a camera's iris is slowly opened or closed to create an expanding or diminishing circular image, ultimately either filling the screen or blacking it out.

■ The iris fade technique was popular in early silent films and animated cartoons.

■ *e.g.* The Cabinet of Doctor Caligari (Robert Wiene, 1919)

**ISP:** see internet service provider.

**ITC:** see Independent Television Commission.

**ITN:** see Independent Television News.

**ITV:** see Independent Television.

**ITV plc:** see Independent Television.

**journalistic licence:** the degree to which it is permissible for journalists to elaborate or exaggerate a story in order to make it more readable or controversial, thus attracting greater attention.

■ The purely factual reporting of news stories would often be of little interest to viewers or readers, therefore journalists usually develop an **angle** to engage an audience. In the case of **tabloid journalism**, this can often result in bending the truth to suit the story.

***J-17*:** magazine launched as *Just Seventeen* in 1983 by Nick Logan, and published by **Emap** until its closure in 2004.

■ *J-17* was targeted at teenage girls aged 12 to 16, who aspired to the age of 17 with its connotations of maturity and excitement.

■ The magazine's contents identified a readership interested in sex, future careers, celebrities, mobile phones, fashion and appearance. It also provided advice on sexual behaviour and relationships and in its day broke new ground with its frank and open discussion of sex.

■ Emap closed *J-17* in 2004 following declining sales and increased competition from a new generation of girl's magazines such as *Bliss* and *Sugar*.

**key concept:** any of the core concepts on which a media studies programme focuses, specifically audience, genre, ideology, institutions, language, narrative and representation.

■ These key concepts provide a systematic structure for the study of the media and media products and provide terms of reference in any media assignment or project. Any analysis of a media topic should be related to the key concepts where appropriate.

**kiss and tell:** popular term for the practice whereby attractive young women seek out sexual relationships with celebrities in order to then sell their story to newspapers or magazines for large sums of money (see celebrity, cheque book journalism).

**knocking copy:** journalistic shorthand for newspaper articles that seek out negative, unflattering or embarrassing events in order to criticise individuals, institutions and organisations in the public eye.

■ *e.g.* The royal family constantly face knocking copy in the tabloid press.

**kung fu:** describes a genre of film, developed in the 1970s around the martial arts, often produced in Hong Kong and associated with the actor/director Bruce Lee.

■ Kung fu movies are essentially narratives built around elaborate and protracted fight scenes (enhanced with special effects) in which a heroic protagonist triumphs in the face of overwhelming odds while in the pursuit of some personal quest.

■ *e.g. Enter the Dragon* (Robert Clouse, 1973)

**lads mag:** lifestyle magazine targeted at young men.

■ The magazines are designed to appeal to stereotypical young men through their emphasis on sexual relationships, good times, partying, entertainment and attractive girls.

■ Lads mags are part of the broad lifestyle magazine genre and deliver audiences of young men to advertisers of cosmetics, clothes, electronic consumer goods and gadgets, motorbikes, cars, holidays and even telephone sex.

■ *e.g. Loaded, FHM, Maxim*

**language:** `key concept` the particular codes used within different media to convey messages to audiences.

■ This includes the content, theme and purpose of a print-based text, its layout and design, the use of written language and of photography and illustration.

■ With the moving image, language involves iconography, *mise en scène*, use of lighting, colour, editing and montage techniques.

■ Visual language involves selection and construction from paradigms to produce syntagms, e.g. a poster, photograph or film.

**langue (French for 'language'):** used as a semiological term by Saussure to mean the code or system from which an act of parole is produced.

■ Parole only has meaning because it is constructed within the system of langue. Semiology explores the relationship between these elements and the construction of signs.

**Lasswell, Harold (1902–78):** US media researcher who identified five key questions to be used as a model (1948) for commencing the investigation of the mass communication process, namely *Who? Says what? In which channel? To whom? With what effect?*

■ Although lacking sophistication and detail, the model remains a useful starting point for investigation.

**lead:** the opening comments of the reporter in a television news report, designed to attract the viewer's attention.

**leader:** the leading (i.e. most important) editorial article in a newspaper.

■ *TIP* Leaders are not to be confused with a lead story, which is the first story or news item in a paper.

**leak:** the unauthorised or unofficial release of secret, restricted or privileged information to the media in such a way as to either reveal official plans unofficially or to subvert official versions of events by releasing embarrassing material.

■ Leaks can work both in favour of those in power and against them, depending on the source of the leak and their motivation.

**left-wing:** having socialist or communist political ideas that advocate change and are critical of the status quo in a society.

**legs:** a term used to describe the stamina or duration of a media product.

■ A news story with legs is one that will continue to attract attention long after its initial impact and which is therefore worth pursuing.

■ A film with legs is one that continues to draw large audiences and to make a profit after the initial impact of its opening.

**Levi-Strauss, Claude (1908–90):** French structuralist anthropologist whose analysis of human culture and myth argued for a common origin for all narratives, based on shared human life experience, fears and expectations.

■ Using the techniques developed by Saussure, Levi-Strauss identified the underlying structures of all myths as being the same. His narrative theory of binary opposition is based on the essential difference between such concepts as culture and nature, the raw and the cooked, good and evil. Narratives are based on oppositional forces and the resolution of conflict. Audiences are positioned on the side that justifies their own cultural values, and resolution reduces underlying anxiety about threats to their way of life.

**libel:** the written publication of malicious or defamatory comments about an individual or organisation, as defined by the law.

■ Britain's libel laws are seen as favouring the rich and powerful who can obtain court injunctions to prevent publication of material they disapprove of and then proceed with libel actions in court. These can result in heavy fines for the publication concerned.

■ *e.g.* In 1992 a libel action was brought by the singer Jason Donovan against the style magazine *The Face* which had suggested he was gay. He was awarded £292,000 but waived the cash since it would have bankrupted the then independent magazine.

**liberal feminism:** a feminist perspective that focuses on the need to change laws to promote equal opportunities and that sees gender inequalities as being the result of the dominant **patriarchal** family model and prejudice.

■ Liberal feminists believe that such developments as equal educational opportunity, more positive media representations and challenges to negative stereotypes in the existing socioeconomic system can end traditional gender-role inequalities and bring lasting change.

**lifestage:** advertising term used in lifestyle analysis, based on the idea that people have different tastes and aspirations at different stages in their lives.

■ *e.g.* dependants (those dependent on other people's money, such as children and students dependent on parents); empty-nesters (adults whose children have left home); pre-family (young couples without children); dinks (dual income/no kids — couples with no children and a large disposable income); grey market

**lifestyle magazine:** any of a broad category of magazines which defines audiences in terms of their consumption of consumer products and way of life.

■ Lifestyle magazines seek to reinforce patterns of consumption and behaviour. They provide audiences with a sense of security and identity, offering advice and providing role models on how to live a particular lifestyle built around the consumption of specific products. Readers' aspirations are stimulated with regard to relationships, possessions, appearance and careers.

■ *e.g.* Gardener's World, More, Smash Hits, Maxim, **Marie Claire**, *Woman's Own, Bizarre, GQ*

■ *TIP* All lifestyle magazines are vehicles for advertisers, who are provided with clear readership profiles.

**lifestyle marketing:** the marketing and advertising of a product by identifying and differentiating patterns of consumption in relation to the lifestyle, tastes and aspirations of particular social groups (see **four Cs**).

**linear narrative:** a sequential narrative with a beginning, a middle and an end — in that order.

■ Linear narratives provide a straightforward, sequential representation of events leading to a single resolution. As such, they are easily accessible to audiences and are the dominant form in **mainstream** media representations.

■ *TIP* Linear narratives are increasingly challenged by the non-linear, which is more reflective of the random experiences of life and the complexity involved in the viewer's construction of meaning, e.g. *Lost Highway* (David Lynch, 1997).

**Lippmann, Walter (1889–1974):** US political philosopher who, in *Public Opinion* (1922) and *The Phantom Public* (1925), raised doubts about the possibility of developing a true democracy in a complex media-dominated society, where elite groups manipulate the masses through **propaganda** into herdlike behaviour and responses.

■ Lippmann was also concerned about the danger of the mass media's use of **stereotypes** as a means of categorising people. He saw stereotypes as negative constructions, simplistic, acquired second-hand rather than based on individual experience, erroneous in nature and resistant to change.

**lip synchronisation (also known as 'lip synching'):** the postproduction practice of adding dubbed dialogue in such a way as to ensure that it coordinates with the lip movements of the actors.

■ Lip synchronisation is characteristic of some production styles; for example, the films of Italian **auteur** Federico Fellini were always dubbed in post-production. The practice detracts from the sense of realism in a film, which in the case of Fellini with his **surrealist** treatments is perhaps not an issue. In other contexts, the crudeness of the practice can detract from the viewing experience.

**log:** a record of a production process, usually involving a brief, an outline of research undertaken, an analysis of the production process and an evaluation or self-assessment of the completed work.

■ *TIP* A log should include dates, decisions and a rationale relating to the whole process, but it should also be a reflective analysis, not just a diary of events.

**long shot:** a distance shot where the camera is a long way from the subject being filmed.

■ A long shot can be effective as an establishing shot that sets the scene for the action and draws in the viewer.

■ *e.g.* The opening of Hitchcock's *Psycho* (1960) is a long shot panning across a city. This slowly transforms into a **zoom** through the window of a hotel room, then to an internal shot of a room and its occupants.

**low-angle shot:** a shot where the camera approaches a subject from below eye level.

■ A low-angle shot can emphasise the size of the object being filmed and add to a point of view perspective.

■ *e.g.* In a *Tom and Jerry* cartoon, the mouse's low-angle view of the cat presents the cat as a towering, threatening monster.

**lowbrow:** describing media texts of low intellectual content, designed primarily for light entertainment.

■ Lowbrow texts demand little from the audience in terms of education or specialist knowledge and are associated with the **dumbing down** of media content.

**low-budget film:** a film made with limited funds, without the backing of a major production company.

■ Low-budget films can be successful if presented effectively to an audience.

■ *e.g.* *The Blair Witch Project* (Daniel Myrick, 1999) cost little to make, being filmed entirely with hand-held cameras in woodland. Cleverly marketed via the internet, in such a way as to create a strong sense of excitement and expectation within the potential audience, it made a fortune for the amateur film makers.

■ *TIP* Low-budget films are usually associated with independent producers and directors.

**low culture**: see lowbrow.

**McGuffin:** a term used by Alfred Hitchcock for a 'red herring' or distracting, irrelevant plot detail, which attracts the viewer's attention away from the main action by appearing to be important but turning out to be irrelevant.

■ *e.g.* the stolen $40,000 dollars in *Psycho* (Alfred Hitchcock, 1960)

**McLuhan, Marshall (1911–80):** Canadian media theorist concerned with evaluating the cultural transformations taking place globally as a result of the development of mass-media technologies.

■ McLuhan was among the first to recognise that the mass media were changing cultural relationships and that the printed word no longer carried the same power.

■ He was famous for memorable one-liners, e.g. 'The medium is the message', meaning that the medium used to communicate strongly affects the message being sent. He changed this phrase to 'The medium is the massage' to convey the power of the media to flatter and persuade.

■ His concept of the **global village** recognised that distances had been rendered insignificant by telecommunications technology.

■ Books: *Understanding Media* (1964), *The Gutenberg Galaxy* (1962)

***Mail on Sunday:*** tabloid Sunday newspaper, owned by **Associated Newspapers**.

■ With **right-wing**, **mainstream**, conservative political views and healthy circulation figures, the paper, with its sister the *Daily Mail*, is seen as a bastion of middle England and **family values** (circulation 2,446,465 January 2005).

**mainstream:** the uncontroversial, generally accepted **attitudes**, **beliefs and values** of the majority population.

■ Mainstream entertainment and media products tend to be family orientated and unchallenging in terms of representation and content.

■ Mainstreamers are individuals who feel comfortable with the status quo and threatened by change.

**male gaze:** term used by Laura **Mulvey** in her essay 'Visual Pleasures and Narrative Cinema' (1975) to describe what she saw as the male point of view adopted by the camera for the benefit of an assumed male audience.

m

■ Mulvey viewed the practice of the camera lingering on women's bodies as evidence that women were being viewed as sex objects for the gratification of men. She argued that the central active characters in films are male and that the male audience identifies with them in their viewing of the passive females. Women in the audience are also positioned by the narrative to identify with the male gaze and see the world through male eyes.

■ Mulvey's essay was hugely influential in the development of **feminist** film studies.

■ *TIP* Mulvey's approach owes much to Freudian psychology. Her arguments can be challenged by simply pointing out that not all central heroic characters in films are male. Also, Mulvey denies the existence of a 'female gaze', which has enjoyed physically attractive men in films from the earliest days of cinema, with stars ranging from Rudolph Valentino to Brad Pitt. Lastly, changes in the representation of women have resulted in fundamental challenges to stereo-typical gender roles since Mulvey's essay was written, e.g. *Kill Bill: Vol. 2* (Quentin Tarantino, 2004).

**Manchester Evening News:** regional newspaper for the Manchester area, part of the **Guardian Media Group** which is itself owned by the Scott Trust.

**manga (from the Japanese for 'comics'):** Japanese adult comic books, popular literature in Japan and respected as an art form.

■ Manga are classified in genres, aimed at different ages and genders and with distinctive covers.

■ Manga, which sometimes depict scenes of a violent or sexual nature, have developed a worldwide market and influence. In their animated film form, they are called **anime**.

**Marie Claire:** women's lifestyle and fashion magazine. The title is owned by **Hachette** of France and published under licence in the USA by the Hearst Corporation, in Britain by **IPC Media** and in Australia by Murdoch Magazines.

■ According to the publishers, *Marie Claire* is aimed at active, independent, fashion-conscious, modern, intelligent, socially aware women between the ages of 20 and 35 and is currently the leading competition to *Cosmopolitan* in the UK.

**marketing:** the transmission of information about a media text to a target audience in such a way as to maximise its appeal to that audience.

■ Marketing is a process designed to ensure the commercial and financial success of a product and a healthy return on money invested.

■ Successful marketing involves strategies based on a detailed knowledge of product and audience and the use of a wide variety of methods to stimulate audience interest.

**marketing mix:** elements that make up the marketing of a product, which include advertising, promotional material, product development and market research.

**Marxism:** ideology derived from the writings of the sociologist Karl Marx (1818–83), which sees society as dominated by capitalist structures which maintain the hegemony of the ruling class and lead to the exploitation of workers.

■ Marxism centres on the concept of economic determinism, which is the belief that economic relationships are the basis for class struggle and result in the suppression of one class by another.

■ Modern Marxists concentrate on the ways in which social institutions such as the media sustain dominant ideology and false consciousness in the interest of the ruling *elite*.

**Marxist feminism:** a feminist perspective which sees capitalism as the principal source of gender inequalities.

■ In a capitalist class hierarchy, women are seen as being subordinate to men and serving the male workforce in terms of low-paid, low-status employment and unpaid domestic labour and child rearing.

■ Domestic violence against women is seen to be the result of the powerless male workforce exercising its frustration on the female sex rather than directing it at the class system.

■ The media and culture industries serve the interests of capitalism by reinforcing traditional gender roles and supporting the status quo created by the dominant ideology.

**mass communication:** the process whereby information is transmitted by means of often complex technology to a large, unspecified audience by a small, cohesive work group with a specific ethos.

**mass culture:** term used by the Marxist Frankfurt School to describe the creation by the mass media of a commercially based popular culture based on trivial and superficial entertainment (see popular culture, highbrow, lowbrow).

**mass media:** the newspaper, magazine, advertising, television, music, radio, cinema and internet industries responsible for the transmission of messages to mass audiences.

■ Mass media content is designed to inform, educate, entertain or persuade members of a target audience.

**master shot:** a camera shot used at the beginning of a sequence to establish the component elements and relationships in such a way as to allow the audience to make sense of the action that follows.

**masthead:** the title of a newspaper as it appears at the top of its front page.

■ The choice of name, typeface, colour and associated display is an important part of a newspaper's ident. Subtle changes to any element can disconcert regular readers who have become familiar and comfortable with their newspaper's identity.

■ The *Daily Telegraph* recently considered dropping the definite article 'the' from its name and decided against it in case its readers were offended.

■ The *Daily Mirror* changed its colour display from red to black to escape its down-market 'red top' label and prior to adopting a more serious tone on international affairs.

■ The *Daily Mail* uses a period gothic font for its title and the royal coat of arms to signal its mainstream, conservative positioning to its readers.

**media:** collective term for the press, broadcast, publishing, music, internet and related industries (see medium).

**media effects theory:** see effects theory.

**media imperialism:** the belief that media industries are used by powerful nations to dominate and control the economic, cultural, political and social systems of weaker countries (see cultural imperialism).

**media language:** see language.

**media saturation:** a state whereby people's experience of the world is dominated by the consumption of media texts.

**mediation:** the means by which, through the use of representation, a media organisation and its employees stand between an event and the public's perception of that event.

■ Mediation involves the process of constructing, interpreting and editing material in accordance with the requirements of the chosen medium of communication.

■ *TIP* It is useful to remember that the term indicates that the media change events by reporting and representing them.

**Mediawatch:** right-wing pressure group and successor to the National Viewers' and Listeners' Association founded by Mary Whitehouse, Mediawatch is similarly pro-censorship and concerned with so-called traditional family values.

**medium (plural media):** any of the various means by which messages are transmitted in mass communication.

■ *e.g.* Print, film and television are visual or audiovisual media, whereas radio and music are audio media.

**merchandising:** the selling of goods associated with the release of a particular film.

■ Merchandising is an important part of the financial strategy of a film launch and its returns add considerably to the financial success of the project.

■ *e.g.* *Jurassic Park* (Steven Spielberg, 1993) merchandise included everything from plastic dinosaurs and T-shirts to children's lunch boxes, computer games, board games, brooches, badges, posters, books and soundtrack recordings.

**message:** the subject matter of an act of communication.

**metanarrative (also known as 'meta discourse'):** postmodernist term used to describe all-embracing social theories, such as **Marxism**, which claim to provide a scientific framework for explaining how societies work.

■ Postmodernists argue that in the fragmented postmodern world, dominated by media-generated artificial realities or **simulcra**, such universal 'big stories' and 'big debates' no longer have validity in explaining the complex and often contradictory forces framing social, cultural and economic relationships.

**method acting:** a style of acting developed by Konstantin Stanislavsky in his book *An Actor Prepares* (1936).

■ Method acting involves actors merging themselves psychologically into the characters they are representing and becoming those characters. The intention is to create the character psychologically and emotionally, as well as physically. The acting is intended to be natural and spontaneous, with actors drawing on their own previously experienced emotions (emotional memory) to match the emotions of the character.

■ Quotation: 'They try not to act but to be themselves, to respond or react', Lee Strasberg (1899–1982), leader of The Actor's Studio.

■ *e.g.* Classic method acting: Marlon Brando's and Rod Steiger's performances in *On the Waterfront* (Elia Kazan, 1954), Robert DeNiro in *Taxi Driver* (Martin Scorsese, 1976) and *Raging Bull* (Martin Scorsese, 1980).

**methodology:** the means or system used to collect and interpret the information used in media research.

**metonym:** part of a representational image used to stand for a whole in such a way that the viewer is able to construct the rest of the story from the part given.

■ Metonyms are an essential part of media texts, which can only ever provide a partial representation of a complex and ever-changing reality.

■ As we read media texts metonymically, the choice of single images used to represent larger events or concepts will have a crucial and powerful effect on our understanding.

■ *e.g.* A smiling policeman helping a child cross a busy road is a metonym for a caring community police force, whereas a photograph of police hitting demonstrators with batons at a demonstration is a metonym for a politically repressive police force. The chosen elements of a movie poster represent the characters and action of the whole film, while a photographic image of an earthquake used in a newspaper represents the whole disaster.

**Metro-Goldwyn-Mayer (MGM):** one of the five largest Hollywood studios during the 1930–48 golden age period, taken over by the Sony Corporation of America in 2005.

■ Founded in 1924, MGM controlled such stars as Judy Garland and Greta Garbo.

■ MGM was one of the last major independent studios before it was taken over in 2005.

**MGM:** see Metro-Goldwyn-Mayer.

**MGN:** see Mirror Group Newspapers.

**midi:** see Berliner.

**mid-market:** demographic term applied to people, products, campaigns, services or media directed at or leaning toward the C1 or C2 social grade (see ABC1 scale).

**Miramax:** a film corporation founded by Harvey and Bob Weinstein in 1979, under the ownership of Walt Disney Studio Entertainment from 1993.

■ Miramax graduated from the production of low-budget, art house movies to more prestigious and financially rewarding mainstream productions.

■ Films produced by Miramax include *Chicago* (Rob Marshall, 2002) and *Gangs of New York* (Martin Scorsese, 2002).

**Mirror Group Newspapers (MGN):** publishing group responsible for the *Daily Mirror*, the *Sunday Mirror* and the *Sunday People*, part of the Trinity Mirror group.

***mise en scène* (French for 'put in the picture/scene'):** the arrangement by a film maker of everything that is to be included in a shot or frame.

■ This includes settings, props, décor, lighting, actors, characters, positioning and all other technical elements which contribute to the look of the scene and create its distinctive quality and unity.

**mixer:** in the music industry, an electronic system for combining sound recorded on different tracks.

**mockumentary:** a satirical, irreverent, parody of documentary technique.

■ *e.g.* Classic film example: *This is Spinal Tap* (Rob Reiner, 1984), a spoof documentary 'diary of a band'.

**model:** an idealised representation of the communication process.

■ Models are explanations in graphic or verbal form of the complex relationships between institutions, media channels, media texts or messages and audiences.

■ Attempts have been made to express the whole complex process in one model but most models concentrate on a single aspect of concern to the model maker.

**mode of address:** in narrative studies, the way in which media texts talk to an audience.

■ In audiovisual texts, this can be in the form of a **voice-over** where an unseen narrator addresses the audience. The narrator could be one of the text's characters and provide insight into what occurs on screen.

■ In *film noir*, the private detective's voice often provides a running commentary on the action, from his perspective.

■ *TIP* Fans of the cult movie *Blade Runner* (Ridley Scott, 1982) dispute which of the two versions of the film, one with lead character Deckard's (Harrison Ford) off-screen narration and one without, is the most successful.

**monopoly:** total control of a commercial market by one company where there is no meaningful competition.

■ Increased concentration of media ownership in the hands of a few multinational corporations (**oligopoly**) has raised concerns about possible monopolies.

■ *TIP* Monopolies are not allowed in the UK and planned company mergers which may create a monopoly must be referred to the Competition Commission (previously known as the Monopolies and Mergers Commission) for approval. Nevertheless, this does not prevent individual companies or groups from holding a dominant market position and attempting to exclude competitors.

■ *e.g.* BT, Britain's largest telecommunications operator, has frequently been accused by its rivals of uncompetitive behaviour and of exploiting its dominant market position by closing its network to other operators. An **Ofcom** ruling in 2005 forced the company to cut prices and allow other operators into the market which will, however, still be dominated by the largest companies.

**montage:** the selecting and piecing together of material for a film, composite photograph or artwork.

■ The process involves placing images next to each other, in a sequence or **syntagm**, to suggest an idea, thereby often creating a sequential narrative.

■ *e.g.* A picture of a dead body followed by a picture of man holding a gun suggests that the man with the gun is the killer.

**moral panic:** concept devised by Jock Young and developed by Stan Cohen to explain the way in which media focus on the behaviour of a social group or an event can be inflated by sensational reporting and the repeated use of **stereotypes**, leading to public overreaction or panic at a supposed threat to society.

■ The key element in moral panic is a feeling that the situation is out of control in some way and therefore represents a threat to the moral order.

m

■ *e.g.* Gangster rap lyrics have been accused of being responsible for an increase in gun crime without any real evidence.

■ *TIP* Moral panic tends to focus on youth subcultures that are seen to be deviant and threatening, usually in relation to a combination of sex, drugs, violence and a general lack of respect for conventional morality. Over 40 years, mods, rockers, hippies, skinheads, goths, punks, rastas and rappers have all been subject to moral panic coverage in the media.

**Morley, David:** professor of communications at Goldsmiths College, London University, whose specialisms include cultural consumption in relation to television, media markets, cultural identities and cultural imperialism.

■ His best-known work, in association with the **Centre for Contemporary Cultural Studies**, is in the field of **reception theory** and was published as *The Nationwide Audience* (1980). The study, which explores the extent to which individual interpretation of programmes might vary in line with sociocultural background, was an important contribution to the development of **active audience theory**. *Nationwide* was an evening current affairs television programme.

**morphing (from 'metamorphosis', meaning to change or be between shapes):** the changing of film character shape achieved through computer technology.

■ Morphing techniques date from early cinema, where cross-fades and **dissolves** were used, e.g. the transformation of kindly Dr Jekyll into the evil Mr Hyde in *Dr Jekyll and Mr Hyde* (Rouben Mamoulian, 1931).

■ Computer-generated morphing has now become an expected feature of **horror** and **science fiction** films and is widely used in television advertisements.

■ *TIP* The underrated and unusual film *The Company of Wolves* (Neal Jordan, 1984), based on the fairy-tale story by Angela Carter, was one of the first films to use computer morphing to change men into beasts.

**motif:** a recurrent theme or element that runs through a film and is repeated in a significant way, often expressing a key message.

■ A motif can be a symbol, an object, a stylistic element, a word or a phrase and is sometimes picked up by the film's publicity material.

■ *e.g.* In *Gladiator* (Ridley Scott, 2000), the repeated scenes where the gladiator Maximus walks dreamily through a wheat field represent his desire to rejoin his family in the afterlife; in *What Lies Beneath* (Robert Zemeckis, 2000), the design on the necklace worn by the dead girl; in *Blade Runner* (Ridley Scott, 1982), the unicorn device.

**MP3:** computer software package which allows a user to convert a music CD track into a computer file and post it on the internet for downloading by others.

■ The implication of MP3 and other similar software, for example, Windows Media Audio (WMA), is that music can be downloaded free of charge.

- Websites such as Napster were created solely for the purpose of allowing free music downloads and the sharing of music files but came up against copyright law. Legal action by music publishing companies against Napster, which created the file-sharing system in 1999, forced the company to close in 2001. It relaunched in 2003 as a legal service charging for music.
- The development poses a problem for the artist and the music industry as copyright law is being broken and neither makes any money from the practice.

**MTV (Music Television):** worldwide music television channel founded in the USA in 1981 and owned by Viacom.

- MTV operates in 136 territories, reaching over 300 million households, and has various versions such as MTV Europe, MTV Mandarin, MTV India, MTV Nordic and MTV Australia. The company claims that it is sensitive to worldwide cultural and musical diversity. In spite of this claim, critics argue that its prime concern is to deliver youth audiences to advertisers and that it promotes essentially Western consumer values.

**multiculturalism:** the recognition that the increasing cultural diversity of Western societies should be acknowledged, supported, encouraged and reflected in all aspects of life, as being both inevitable and also socially and economically desirable.

- Legislation requires the equal treatment of all cultures, regardless of ethnicity and beliefs.
- Media representations increasingly reflect the growing diversity of British society.
- *TIP* Some ethnic and religious minorities, who insist on retaining their own separate identity, may find that the terms of their own beliefs make it difficult for them to tolerate and accept all aspects of cultural diversity, e.g. in relation to gender equality, religious belief and sexuality.

**multimedia:** the term used to describe computer systems that support the combination of text, video, graphics and sound in an integrated way. Multimedia implies the coming together of previously diverse systems and their integration into computer systems via CD-ROM (compact disc readable by a computer) and DVD drives. The term also covers interactive television and MP3 players (computer devices for playing music files).

**multinational:** a large company that operates beyond national boundaries.

- Multinational companies are part of the process of globalisation and reflect both vertical and horizontal integration of media industries on a global scale.

**multiplex:** a large cinema complex that operates several screens showing different films under one roof.

- Multiplexes were developed in the 1980s as a means of showing a large number of films to family audiences to generate large box office takings. They have developed as **mainstream** family entertainment centres, with fast food restaurants and coffee bars attached.

■ Major multiplex owner UCI has now merged with Odeon under the ownership of finance company Terra Firma, with 40% of all UK cinemas. Also UGC, the largest European cinema operator, was bought out by the UK cinema chain Cineworld in 2004. Both developments have resulted in the increasing concentration of cinema ownership.

■ Multiplexes rarely show **independent** or **art house** films.

**Mulvey, Laura (1941–):** feminist academic and media and film critic, responsible for developing theories of the **male gaze** in her 1975 essay 'Visual Pleasure and Narrative Cinema'.

**Murdoch, Rupert (1931–):** chairman of the **News Corporation** and one of the most powerful figures in the media world.

■ Australian by birth, Murdoch was born into a family with newspaper publishing interests. He arrived on the British media scene in 1969 with his purchase of the *Sun* newspaper from Reed International. He has expanded his newspaper holdings to cover one third of all daily and Sunday newspapers sold in the UK. His companies, under the corporate title the News Corporation, represent one of the three largest media holdings in the world.

■ Murdoch's company has worldwide media interests from **BSkyB** and HarperCollins publishers in Britain to Fox TV, Fox News, **Twentieth Century Fox** film studios, numerous sports channels, and the *New York Post* newspaper all in the USA. The company also has large holdings in Australia, with a major stake in regional newspaper ownership and publishing interests. News Corporation claims to be the only **vertically integrated** media company producing and distributing television, cable, film, and satellite productions on five continents.

**musical:** a film **genre** that incorporates songs as part of the film's **narrative**.

■ The genre has proved versatile, adapting to different musical tastes and changes in expectation.

■ *e.g.* Classic musicals through the decades include: *Top Hat* (Mark Sandrich, 1935), *The Wizard of Oz* (Victor Fleming, 1939), *Oklahoma!* (Fred Zinneman, 1955), *The King and I* (Walter Lang, 1956), *West Side Story* (Robert Wise, 1961), *Sweet Charity* (Bob Fosse, 1969), *Cabaret* (Bob Fosse, 1972), *Saturday Night Fever* (John Badham, 1977), *Moulin Rouge* (Baz Luhrmann, 2001) and *Chicago* (Rob Marshall, 2002).

**myth:** in contemporary society, a persistent belief based on the constant repetition of particular representations by the media and of importance in the way in which a culture views itself.

■ In Roland **Barthes**'s orders of signification, myth is part of the second and most complex order. Established cultural myths become deeply embedded, sometimes working on a subconscious level and therefore proving difficult to challenge or alter.

■ Myths are used to structure representations in texts. In advertising, for example, the countryside is used mythically as a setting for products seeking to represent themselves as healthy, wholesome, traditional, reliable and of good quality, e.g. Baxter's soups, Anchor butter.

■ *e.g.* The Germans make good cars; the French are good cooks; women are bad drivers; America is a land of opportunity.

■ *TIP* Myths are neither true nor false, nor are they subjective **stereotypes**; they are an underpinning set of cultural assumptions that structure our reading of media texts.

**narrative:** `key concept` the story line and structure of a media text.
- Narratives or stories help to shape and explain all aspects of our lives from earliest infancy. They are part of the way in which we make sense of the world and provide reassurance in the face of the dangers and contradictions of everyday experience.
- Narratives are structured within genres, which provide frameworks of expectation, predictability and outcome.

**narrative theory:** a type of thinking that seeks to explain narrative structures and their relationship to wider cultural and genre-related factors.
- Narrative theorists seek to deconstruct narratives in order to identify their common characteristics and component elements, e.g. Todorov, Levi-Strauss, Barthes, Propp.

**narrator:** an individual who tells the story in film and television productions, sometimes as a voice-over.
- A narration can be in the first person (I, We) or in the third person (He, They), depending on whether it is subjective and involved or objective and detached.

**narrowcasting:** the targeting of a small, carefully defined social group for a media product; the opposite of broadcasting.
- Multichannel television allows for narrowcasting in line with viewer interest, e.g. The History Channel.

**national newspaper:** a newspaper that reflects national rather than regional concerns, is distributed across the whole country and is printed in various locations, usually including London.

**National Union of Journalists (NUJ):** the principal trade union to which most journalists belong.
- Part of the NUJ's role is to act as a pressure group promoting the interests of journalists, in particular in the often difficult world of libel laws and the

protection of sources of information, where individual journalists may find themselves facing legal challenges.

**National Viewers' and Listeners' Association:** a pro-censorship pressure group, now called **Mediawatch**, founded by Mary **Whitehouse** in 1965.

**NC:** see News Corporation

**negotiated reading:** a reading of a text which assumes that no absolute meaning exists and that meaning is generated and negotiated by what the reader brings to the text in terms of attitudes, beliefs, values and experience.

■ The term is part of Stuart Hall's encoding/decoding model along with dominant and oppositional readings (see reception theory).

■ *TIP* A negotiated reading emphasises the position of the subject or audience member.

**new ladism:** term applied to the male backlash against feminism and girl power, as exemplified by the values represented in magazines such as *Loaded, FHM* and *Maxim*.

**new man:** a term used to describe a new type of masculinity identified and developed by advertising media in the 1980s in line with lifestyle marketing strategies.

■ The new man was said to be sensitive and caring, happy to share household responsibilities and in touch with his emotions. While clearly a response to the greater social and career equality existing between men and women, the new man was largely a media creation.

■ *e.g.* Advertising campaigns showed men in domestic and childcare roles, alongside career women in dominant roles.

**New Musical Express (NME):** a weekly UK music magazine founded in 1952, now known as the *NME* and published by IPC Media.

■ The *NME* is the most important and long-lasting UK music magazine and has chronicled the most significant developments in popular music over 50 years. The paper was responsible for introducing the UK's first record listings chart in the early 1950s and was the first music magazine to launch an internet site in the 1990s.

■ Circulation in the 1970s reached 300,000 but fell in the 1980s to a low of 85,000. This led to a publicity campaign in 1998 using local press to help restore the publication's grass roots and regional credibility and to ward off potential competition from Emap publications.

■ The title incorporated rival *Melody Maker* (founded in 1926 and published by the same company) in 2001 and has re-established a circulation of 117,000 copies, together with its reputation as Britain's leading music magazine.

■ The *NME* has been an important career springboard for journalists including Nick Logan, Nick Kent, Roy Carr, Tony Parsons and Julie Burchill.

**news agency (also known as 'press agency'):** organisation responsible for gathering and distributing news to subscribers, usually broadcasters, newspapers and periodicals.

**News Corporation (NC):** parent company of Rupert Murdoch's global media empire.

■ News Corporation has worldwide interests in film-making, broadcasting, print and electronic media.

**News International:** subdivision of News Corporation, responsible for newspaper publication in the UK.

■ Company titles include the *Sun, The Times, The Sunday Times* and the *News of the World.*

**News of the World:** popular Sunday tabloid with the largest circulation of any British newspaper (3,823,000 January 2005).

■ The *News of the World* is part of Rupert Murdoch's News International organisation and is renowned for its combination of sex, soap opera, sleaze, and celebrity story-lines with a populist, right-wing agenda.

**newspaper readership:** see readership.

**newsprint:** the paper on which newspapers are printed.

**news values:** term used by researchers to describe the various criteria involved in the selection of news by broadcasters and journalists.

■ News values were first identified by Galtung and Ruge in the early 1960s and their list has since been adapted by others. The following is a composite, comprehensive list:
  ● frequency: news needs to happen on a daily and frequent basis to meet schedules
  ● cultural proximity: news need to be close to home or related to home issues
  ● threshold: news needs to be of sufficient importance to attract attention; big events get noticed more than small ones
  ● negativity: bad news has priority over good news
  ● predictability: news tends to anticipate and justify expected outcomes
  ● unexpectedness: news has to seem unexpected, even though most of it takes place within predictable patterns
  ● continuity: follow-up elements of a big story are seen as newsworthy
  ● unambiguity: events with a clear meaning are more likely to be reported than complex issues

- composition: news is subject to editorial construction and reflects individual editorial choices, the constraints of the medium and organisational values
- personalisation: events which can be made personal get priority
- reference to elite nations: powerful, mostly Western nations have priority coverage
- reference to elite persons: celebrities get more coverage than unknown persons
- narrativisation: news is constructed as a story and all elements of narrative theory apply
- visual imperative: television news and tabloid journalism tend to be driven by pictures and what is available

**niche marketing:** the targeting of a small but significant group of consumers with a media product directed specifically at their interests.

■ *e.g.* *Living France* magazine is directed at people who have a specific interest in the French way of life, in holidaying in France and who may have a second home there.

**nodding shot:** see reaction shot.

**noise:** term, originating in telecommunications, for any interference with the communication process. The term is now used to describe anything which interferes with the communication process or confuses an audience with multiple messages.

■ Researcher Claude Shannon devised (1948) what he called a mathematical model to explain how disruption or interference with the telecommunication process — what he called disruption noise — could be measured and eliminated.

■ *e.g.* During a general election campaign, too many conflicting or competing stories about policies may constitute noise by confusing electors and diverting attention away from the issues that politicians seek to highlight.

**non-linear editing:** the editing of video, digital and film products using a computer software package that allows editors to access material instantaneously rather than sequentially.

**non-linear narrative:** see linear narrative.

**non-narrative television:** a television text that seems to present reality to the viewer, for example, sport, news and games shows, rather than using conventional narrative structures.

■ In spite of their non-narrative appearance, many of these texts are increasingly packaged using traditional narrative forms and expectations. Game shows are a quest or journey (**Propp**) to a promised land of wealth and plenty, and

**n**

'weakest links' are rejected in a struggle for dominance. **Binary oppositions** are structured into football reporting, and character sketches of team members and their roles allow viewers to identify with them during the contest, often as heroes and villains (Propp). Similarly, equilibrium disruption (**Todorov**) and the struggle for resolution is present in many sport and news reports.

**norms:** culturally determined, value-based rules of the type of behaviour expected in different social situations.
- Norms can vary over time and reflect the values of different cultures or subcultures. Conformity to norms can be a source of security for group members and the challenging or breaking of norms can be seen as disruptive of social order.
- **Mainstream** media, in adopting moral positions, can often signal whether or not norms are being broken. For example, tabloid newspaper coverage of the behaviour of **opinion leaders** and role models (e.g. football celebrities) in relation to sex, drink, drugs and violent behaviour can be an indicator both of the level of public tolerance and of where the line is drawn before behaviour is judged 'out of order'.
- *e.g.* David Beckham's alleged affair, Wayne Rooney's alleged sexual antics, and Paul Gascoigne's (Gazza's) alleged drinking and domestic violence.

**Northern and Shell:** media company, under the chairmanship of Richard Desmond, which owns a wide range of lifestyle magazines, including *OK* and various soft pornography titles, together with Express Newspapers, publishers of the *Daily Express* and *Sunday Express*.

**not crossing the line:** see 180-degree rule.

**Nouvelle Vague:** see French New Wave.

**NUJ:** see National Union of Journalists.

**objectivity:** the presentation of a media text from a neutral or objective standpoint, without individual or institutional bias and without the deliberate preferment of one viewpoint over another.

■ Stuart Hall has argued that objectivity is 'an operational fiction' given the in-built institutional biases involved in the production of media texts, and that dominant ideology is always represented as common sense or objectivity.

■ *TIP* Although it sounds fair and reasonable, total objectivity, even if possible, may not always be desirable. To be objective, is it necessary to balance racist and non-racist views or pro-terrorist and anti-terrorist views?

**Obscene Publications Act:** nineteenth-century legislation, amended in 1959 and 1964, used as the legal basis for the confiscation and destruction of all media texts deemed obscene under the terms of the Act (usually those that are sexual in content) and the prosecution of those responsible for their publication, distribution or sale.

■ Obscenity is defined as 'likely to deprave and corrupt' and is difficult to prove in a changing moral climate. The trial in 1961 of *Lady Chatterley's Lover* (D. H. Lawrence), in which Penguin books succeeded in defending the literary merit of the novel, was seen as a landmark in the struggle against censorship.

■ Although still on the statute book, the Act is rarely used because of the difficulty in obtaining convictions.

**Observer:** a Sunday quality broadsheet newspaper with left-of-centre politics.

■ Established in 1791, the *Observer* is one of the oldest media publications in Britain. It is currently owned by the Guardian Media Group (circulation 446,818 copies, January 2005).

**Ofcom:** the public body responsible for regulating the television, radio and telecommunications media in Britain.

■ Ofcom replaced the Independent Television Commission, the Broadcasting Standards Council, the Radio Authority and the Radio Communications Agency under the terms of the 2003 Communications Act.

**O**

- Ofcom's remit does not currently (2005) include the BBC.
- Complaints to Ofcom about media content tend to be about offence caused by language, sexual portrayal and violence, where the regulator is particularly concerned to monitor the 9 p.m. watershed, and also religious offence, accuracy and impartiality. The regulator publishes regular Ofcom Broadcast Bulletins with details of complaints, the responses of broadcasters and conclusions.

***OK!*:** a celebrity-focused lifestyle magazine owned by Northern and Shell, established in competition with market leader *Hello!*.

**oligarchy:** a political system wherein power is exercised by a small elite group, usually in its own interests.

**oligopoly:** the control of a market by a small number of firms which are in a position to fix prices and restrict the entry of new competition.
- The dominance currently exercised by giant globalised media corporations and the tendency toward ever larger conglomerates has created an oligopoly in the production and distribution of media products.

**180-degree rule (also known as 'not crossing the line'):** the film-making rule of placing the camera in a 180-degree relationship with the filmed subject to ensure narrative continuity.

**open question:** a question which allows an interviewee to develop his or her point of view and to expand on a subject.
- *e.g.* Would you please tell us more about your experience of working at Tesco?

**opinion leader:** an individual who by virtue of his or her status or popularity within a society is seen as having an influential role in shaping public opinion on a subject.
- Traditionally, opinion leaders were seen to be those in moral or political authority, members of the church, politicians and civic leaders, academics and industrialists. In contemporary popular culture, pop stars, celebrities, models and sports idols are more likely to be chosen to lead advertising or public information campaigns.

**oppositional reading (also known as 'aberrant decoding'):** a reading of a media text that rejects the ideological positioning and apparent meaning intended by the producers of the text and substitutes a radical alternative.
- The term, along with negotiated reading and dominant reading, is part of Stuart Hall's encoding /decoding model (see reception theory).

**Oscars, the:** see Academy Awards.

**out take:** a film shot rejected and omitted from the final cut of a film.

**package (1):** in television journalism, a short television news report, usually between 80 and 105 seconds long, shot on location and submitted by the reporter to his or her news organisation.

**package (2):** in film, all the marketing elements, including concept, script, director, stars and locations, which make the project a viable and coherent financial proposition.

**pan:** camera action involving gently moving the camera 180 degrees across the subject matter in a horizontal plane.

**paparazzi:** a term used to describe press photographers who aggressively pursue and harass public figures and celebrities in search of candid and often compromising photographs.
- The term comes from the name of the society photographer in Federico Fellini's film *La Dolce Vita* (1960) and may originate from the Sicilian for 'oversized mosquito'.
- Paparazzi were accused of causing the deaths in 1997 of Princess Diana and Dodi Fayed in a car crash in Paris during a high-speed pursuit of the couple.

**paradigm:** term developed by **Saussure** and **Barthes** to describe the cultural set or category from which one element may be chosen in the construction of a **syntagm** or chain of meaning.
- *e.g.* A woman's wardrobe contains a range of paradigms, for example, one each for blouses, jumpers, skirts, dresses, trousers, jeans, jackets and shoes. When she dresses in the morning, the woman can choose only one element from some of these paradigms to make up her outfit for the day. If she changes any element, then the syntagm — her overall appearance and look in this context — will also change. In the same way, paradigmatic choices involved in the composition of a poster (for example, colour, typeface, anchoring caption, photographic images, setting) will fundamentally affect the syntagmatic whole.

**parallel action:** the narrative technique of showing two or more scenes happening at the same time by cutting between them.

■ *e.g.* the closing scenes of *The Godfather Part III* (Francis Ford Coppola, 1990)

**parody:** the imitation of one media text by another for comic effect.

■ *e.g.* *Blazing Saddles* (Mel Brooks, 1974) parodies all the iconographic, narrative and character features of the Western genre; *Scary Movie* (Keenan Ivory Wayans, 2000) parodies the horror genre

**parole (French for 'speech'):** used as a semiological term by Saussure to mean a particular act of language, such as a spoken utterance, a poster or even a novel, constructed according to the rules of the langue from which it is drawn.

**passive audience theories:** theories that see audiences as passive recipients of media output.

■ Passive theories tend to see audience behaviour as directly affected by media content and theorists are concerned to measure these effects, particularly with regard to the effects of media portrayals of sex and violence.

■ *e.g.* cultivation theory, hypodermic theory, effects theory, dependency theory

**pastiche:** a media text made up of pieces from other texts or of imitations of other styles.

■ The term is often used to describe an unoriginal, derivative text but it can be used positively if the pastiche involves a deliberate homage to other works.

**patriarchy:** male domination of the political, cultural and socioeconomic system.

■ Under patriarchy, male perspectives and male achievements are valued and rewarded at the expense of the female. Female contributions to society are ignored and women are culturally and economically invisible, being defined solely by their relation to men.

■ Patriarchy is an important assumption behind some feminist film criticism, which sees the male domination of film discourse as evidenced in the male gaze.

**PCC:** see Press Complaints Commission.

**Pearson:** international media company, owner of the *Financial Times*, Longmans publishers, Penguin Books and the Viking Press, and with many other media interests including a share in Five (formerly Channel 5) television.

**periodical:** a publication appearing at regular intervals, usually weekly or monthly, containing articles, stories, pictures and features focused on a particular area of interest.

■ *e.g.* Political periodicals include *Time Magazine*, the *New Statesman* and *The Economist*.

**persuasion:** the intention demonstrated by an external agency or organisation to alter the attitudes, beliefs, values and behaviour of a targeted social group.

■ Those seeking to persuade include advertisers, politicians and religious leaders, and the means they employ may be advertising or political or public information campaigns.

■ *e.g.* The government has initiated public information campaigns on health issues such as the spread of the AIDS virus and the dangers of smoking.

**photojournalism:** the use of photographs as journalism, where a picture or a series of pictures is used to tell a story, often anchored by a caption which encourages a preferred reading of the image.

■ Single-image photographs with appropriate captions often form the front pages of tabloid newspapers.

■ *e.g.* Photographic images of the Vietnam War (ended 1975) printed in publications such as *Life* magazine created powerful iconic images of that war and helped change public opinion in the USA, e.g. the work of photographer Don McCullin in Vietnam.

**photomontage:** the placing together of different photographs so as to construct a new text.

■ Elements of photographs may be cropped and placed together to create meaning not present or intended when the original images were made.

**Pierce, Charles (1839–1914):** US semiologist, working in the philosophical academic tradition, who developed categories of the sign identified by Saussure and applied them to 'social constructs' other than language.

■ Pierce introduced the terms icon, index and symbol to describe the relationship between the sign and its object (that to which it refers).

■ An iconic sign is one that resembles its object or looks and sounds like it, e.g. a photograph.

■ An indexical sign is one that points to its object, e.g. the Eiffel tower is an icon of Paris.

■ A symbolic sign is one whose object is a matter of convention and agreement, e.g. the red cross as a symbol of medical aid.

**pilot:** a trial sample of a potential television programme or series, produced to judge public reaction and test viability.

**pirate radio:** an illegal radio station operating off the coast of Britain (on a boat, hence 'pirate') outside national territorial waters and therefore beyond the reach of restrictive broadcasting laws in force during the early 1960s.

■ The music output of the British Broadcasting Corporation (BBC) in the early 1960s did not cater adequately for a teenage audience interested in the expanding world of rock and pop. Apart from the traditional BBC Light

Programme, listeners had only the commercial Radio Luxemburg, broadcasting from Europe, as an alternative. The pirates filled this gap in the market and demonstrated through their style and content the future of music radio.

■ Legislation allowing commercial stations to operate (1974) and reform of the BBC, with the establishment of Radio 1 to replace the Light Programme (1967), made the pirate stations redundant and many of their disc jockeys found work with the BBC.

**pitch:** the case for a television production, film or advertising campaign put forward by its creators to those responsible for commissioning or buying it.

■ A pitch is designed to be persuasive and is delivered with conviction and enthusiasm.

**Pixar:** digital animation company, maker of *Toy Story* (John Lasseter, 1995), *Monsters, Inc.* (Peter Docter, 2001) and *Finding Nemo* (Andrew Stanton and Lee Unkrich, 2003).

■ Pixar was involved in a distribution deal with Disney, which ended in 2004 to allow the company greater independence.

■ *Toy Story* (John Lasseter, 1995) was a landmark production breaking new ground in the use of computer-generated imagery technology.

**pixel:** one picture element of a screen.

■ In colour screens, a pixel is made up of three subpixels: red, green and blue. An average computer screen contains around 78,000 pixels in a vertical and horizontal configuration.

**pixelation:** a stop-motion animation technique where, by exposing single frames of film, the objects or people being filmed are made to move in a jerky and disjointed fashion.

**plasma screen:** a television viewing screen with enhanced image quality, a larger vertical and horizontal (160 degree) viewing angle and which is glare free.

■ Plasma screens are constructed of two thin panels of mounted glass comprised of networks of tiny pockets of compressed gas or pixels. Each pixel contains three subpixels made up of red, green, and blue phosphors. These same colours are found on all cathode ray tube (CRT) devices, such as conventional televisions and computer monitors.

■ In a plasma screen, each subpixel is controlled by electronics to produce over 16 million colours. When an electrical current is applied to a pixel, the gas reacts to form plasma, which then produces ultraviolet light. The light reacts with the coloured phosphors and enhances the flat screen to produce higher-contrast ratios and a better, more realistic picture. Since all the pixels emit light at the same time, the viewer never sees a flickering screen.

**pleasure:** a motivating factor in the consumption of media texts.

■ Pleasure has often been ignored by researchers seeking to explain the motivation of audiences but is reflected in uses and gratifications theory and is an increasing feature of the appeal media products have in a hedonistic, self-gratifying and consumption-orientated cultural environment.

**plot:** those elements of a media text that convey information about the narrative.

■ Plot information includes character detail and behaviour and explanations of a course of events through time.

**pluralism:** the view that where a society is comprised of a wide range of social and ethnic groups with different values, political and ideological beliefs, representations by the media will naturally reflect this diversity.

■ Pluralist models of the media suggest that, with a large number of organisations producing a wide variety of media texts, audiences and readers have total freedom of choice as to what they consume. This approach is challenged by the Marxist emphasis on economic determinism.

■ *TIP* Pluralist models can be criticised as being idealised in that they assume all opinions are given equal weighting and do not attach sufficient importance to power structures and the influence of dominant ideology.

**point-of-view shot (POV):** a camera shot taken from the position of a subject, used to enhance a sense of realism and audience involvement in the action.

**political correctness:** the practice of challenging and altering language that could give offence, stereotype or exclude people because of their disability, race, gender, sexual orientation, religion or political views.

■ The concept was based on the hypothesis of linguists Edward Sapir and Benjamin Whorf that language influences thought, and therefore sexist and racist language promotes sexist and racist thought.

■ Political correctness evolved from the liberation movements in the USA in the 1970s, which challenged the injustices of discrimination. The concept has since expanded to include support for broad social, political and educational change designed to redress injustices and promote multiculturalism.

■ Media representations are an important aspect of political correctness, with concepts of positive and negative representations being central to the debate. Consequently, all mainstream print and broadcast media check language use for political correctness, for example, disabled for crippled, fire fighter for fireman, police officer for policeman, Native American for Indian, chairperson for chairman, visually handicapped for blind.

■ *TIP* Critics argue that a well-meaning intention to promote equality has been oversimplified and misused by politicians, with results that make people feel too sensitive and uneasy with each other and their use of language. Taken to an extreme, it can be seen as a new conformist orthodoxy that is repressive of alternative opinion.

**polysemic:** describes a sign for which there are many possible interpretations and meanings dependent on individuals' social, cultural and educational backgrounds.

**pop music:** technically, any music that reflects popular culture but usually applied to the development of rock and roll from the 1950s to its present widely diverse variations.

■ *TIP* Pop music in all its forms can be a useful focus for the study of the key concept of media studies.

**popular culture:** the culture of ordinary people created and disseminated by the media through film, television, magazines and newspapers (see mass culture).

■ Popular culture was once dismissed as commercially driven, directed at the masses, lowbrow and lacking in serious content. However, since it has become the dominant media-driven culture of Western societies, it is increasingly difficult to distinguish between low and high culture, between popular and mass culture and even between advertising and art (see lowbrow, highbrow).

■ The adjustment of high culture forms, such as fine art, orchestral music, opera, ballet and theatre, to appeal to larger audiences may be termed dumbing down, where intellectually demanding content is made easier to understand and more broadly entertaining.

**pornography:** the representation in print, audiovisual or electronic media of sexual acts regarded as indecent.

■ Soft pornography involves portrayal of the naked human body, often in simulated sexual acts. Hard pornography involves images of human genitals and penetrative sex.

■ Attitudes toward pornography vary widely by generation and culture; even the representation of nudity is unacceptable in Islamic societies. Tolerance of soft pornography and the regulation of hard pornography have become features of contemporary Western societies, while the growth of the internet has lead to a far wider audience for pornographic images than was previously the case.

■ In Western societies, concern is now focused on indecent images of children and their availability on internet sites. Such concerns, relating to child abuse and the encouragement of paedophilia, have led to a legal clampdown on these sites and the arrest of those visiting them.

■ The pornographic video and DVD industry has become one of the largest media industries in California and serves a worldwide market.

**positioning:** the locating of a media product in a market place with regard to audience and socioeconomic, political and cultural factors.

■ *e.g.* Five (formerly Channel 5) television was positioned to aim at a 'modern mainstream' young audience and this was reflected in its presentation of news programmes and its choice of presenters. The *Daily Express* newspaper has recently shifted its political positioning away from New Labour in order to adopt a stance more critical of government.

**post-colonialism:** the condition in which former colonies find themselves as they struggle toward a national and ethnic identity in the face of their colonial cultural legacy and the continuing dominance of Western media and cultural imperialism.

■ The post-colonial experience involves challenging the language, discourse and identities constructed during the colonial period, voicing the sense of disempowerment and cultural humiliation that colonialism created and creating a new independent voice.

■ The expression of a new identity can involve the development of positive representations in literature, drama and film.

■ *e.g.* the creation of a national cinema by individual African states. In some parts of Africa formerly ruled by France, the rejection of the French language and the adoption of English as a world language is seen as one means of rejecting the colonial past.

**post-feminism:** part of the postmodern perspective which takes the achievements of feminism for granted and views it as ineffective in explaining the current condition of women and the many identity choices they face.

**postmodernism:** literally meaning 'after the modern', an aesthetic paradigm that explores the media-saturated, transnational culture of consumption where globalised media corporations provide a universal package of information and entertainment.

■ The term is also important as a description of generic variation in media texts and as a definition of a cultural attitude. Postmodern texts do not follow traditional narrative or genre expectations and may involve a bricolage of elements, often with ambiguous ideological positions and ambivalent endings that challenge the relationship between text and audience.

■ *e.g. Blade Runner* (Ridley Scott, 1982) is a classic early postmodern film. The films of Quentin Tarantino are usually described as postmodern, for example *Kill Bill: Vols. 1* and *2* (2003–04) which mix cultural elements from the American west, traditional Japan and the simulated world of Japanese manga and anime.

**postproduction:** the process of editing and assembling the final version of an audiovisual product to make it ready for distribution or transmission.

■ Postproduction includes adding sound, special effects and graphics.

**p**

**POV:** see point-of-view shot.

**power:** the exercising of control by certain groups over others in society, through means of economic, social, cultural and ideological dominance, in order to achieve their own aims and interests even in the face of opposition.
- Power is reinforced by dominant ideology and by mainstream media content.

**power elite:** in Western capitalist societies, an oligarchy made up of interconnected groups — military, industrial and political — which exercise power in their own interests.

**power structure:** the system through which elite groups in society exercise power.

**PR:** see public relations.

**preferred reading:** the meaning of a text as intended by the author.
- The term is associated with the work of Stuart Hall and David Morley and the view that texts can have open or various meanings or closed, restricted meanings depending on their origin, intention and complexity. Readers, however, can always interpret texts in line with their own attitudes, beliefs and values.
- Preferred readings are often in line with dominant ideology, but resistance to this can generate negotiated or oppositional readings (see reception theory).
- *e.g.* A photograph of a topless female model in a tabloid newspaper might be accepted by a male audience member as an entertaining picture of a desirable attractive girl (preferred), viewed by his girlfriend with an attitude of disapproval but acceptance (negotiated) but rejected by a feminist as an unacceptable, degrading image involved in the exploitation of women as sex objects for male enjoyment (oppositional).

**prejudice:** the pre-judging of an issue or social group, usually in a negative or stereotypical way.
- Prejudice often involves the targeting of vulnerable minority groups viewed as not conforming to mainstream norms or expectations in some way. Groups identified and stereotyped by tabloid newspapers in this way can often face prejudice as a result, e.g. ethnic minorities, homosexuals, asylum seekers.

**prequel:** a film which narrates events that took place prior to the story enacted in a previously released film, using many of the same characters.
- *e.g. Star Wars: Episode I – The Phantom Menace* (George Lucas, 1999) — the first Star Wars movie appeared in 1977.

**press agency:** see news agency.

**press baron:** any of various powerful owners of newspapers from the early 1900s through to the 1960s.

■ *e.g.* Lords Northcliffe and Rothermere, owners of the *Daily Mail*; Lord Beaverbrook, owner of Express Newspapers until 1964; Cecil Harmsworth King, head of the International Publishing Corporation, publisher of the *Daily Mirror* until 1970

**Press Complaints Commission (PCC):** newspaper complaints body or 'watchdog', established in 1991 to monitor newspaper content in response to criticism by members of the public.

■ The commission is intended to provide recourse for those who feel that newspaper content has either offended or misrepresented them personally, or who have a view about fairness or ethical nature of newspaper content. It operates under a 16-point code of practice and if, after investigating a complaint, the commission finds a newspaper is at fault, it can require the paper to publish details of the judgement.

■ *e.g.* The PCC was involved in discussions with national newspapers to protect princes William and Harry from excessive intrusion during their university years.

■ *TIP* The commission has often faced the criticism that it does not have sufficient authority and powers, so that those ordinary members of the public with serious grievances about their treatment in the press are still obliged to take costly legal action.

**press corps:** the various members of the international press who follow public figures as part of an entourage, attend press briefings and report back to their various organisations.

**press kit:** an assembly of still photographs, video clips, cast details, plot synopsis and publicity spin, offered to newspaper and magazine journalists by film distributors as part of the marketing strategy before the release of a film.

**press release:** a prepared statement released to the press for publication.

■ Press releases are often written and presented in such a way as to resemble reported news. They are issued on behalf of individuals or organisations and are designed to represent and explain their activities in a positive way. They are useful to newspapers since they are ready-made journalism, can be easily adapted or absorbed into broader articles and they fill space.

**pressure group:** a political-interest group formed by like-minded people to exert influence on politicians, public figures and the media in the advancement of their cause or beliefs, with the intention of influencing public policy.

■ *e.g.* Mediawatch, the pro-censorship group; Liberty, the civil rights group; Greenpeace, the environmental campaign group; the Countryside Alliance, the pro-hunting and traditional country life group

■ *TIP* In recent years, special-interest groups and religious groups arguing for greater recognition of their specific values and beliefs have become more active and significant, e.g. The Muslim Council of Britain (founded 1997).

**preview:** the pre-release showing of a film to selected members of the target audience, including film critics, to gain feedback on the film's likely reception.

■ Previews can be used to generate critical interest and press reviews of a film prior to general release. They can also be used at an earlier stage of the production process to assess likely public reaction to the film and to allow for final edit adjustments in line with feedback, which might make the film more popular and commercially successfully.

**primary research:** research undertaken through direct interview with a source or by direct access to original, unmediated documents or images.

■ Primary research includes content analysis.

■ *TIP* The analysis of a media text, such as a film, television programme or magazine, undertaken as part of an essay or project, is classed as primary research.

**prime time:** 7.30 p.m.–10.30 p.m., the period of time with the largest number of television viewers and, on commercial channels, the period of time when most advertising revenue is earned.

■ *e.g.* *EastEnders*, with high viewing figures, is shown during a prime-time slot.

***Private Eye*:** satirical magazine founded in 1962 by Peter Cook, Richard Ingrams and Christopher Booker.

■ *Private Eye* has become a British institution and, having survived numerous libel actions, continues to print a mixture of comic satire, cartoons and more serious 'insider' articles revealing the seamy side of British political life.

**process model:** a view which sees mass communication as a series of stages in a linear process from sources to destinations.

■ Process models tend to be linear in form and attempt to breakdown individual elements of communication into processes that can be studied.

■ The process model emphasises the different elements that enable the transmission of messages from sources to destinations. These include a source, a sender, encoding the message, a channel, a medium, a receiver and a destination.

■ Some process models also allow for feedback and interference (noise) but do not consider the cultural context of mass communication emphasised by semiology.

■ *e.g.* Shannon and Weaver's (1948) mathematical model has the following elements: *source–message–transmitter–signal/noise/received signal–receiver–message–destination*.

■ *TIP* Process models can be contrasted with semiological models where the emphasis is on how meaning is created as a result of interaction between creators and consumers of texts, and on the signs used in their construction.

**producer:** in films, the person responsible for organising the financing, location, casting and shooting of a film; in television, the person who, working alongside writers, directors and actors, develops ideas and shapes them into a programme.

- A film producer develops the script and also manages personnel relations, including hiring and firing members of the crew.
- A television producer researches, plans, produces, and directs specific television programming, manages and directs the production crew, provides technical expertise during production and manages the completion of the programme, including editing.

**production company:** company responsible for making television programmes.

- In a deregulated media environment, independent production companies are responsible for the making of an increasing number of programmes, which are commissioned by and sold to broadcast companies such as the British Broadcasting Corporation and Channel 4.
- *e.g.* Hat Trick Productions makes *Have I Got News For You*, *Drop the Dead Donkey* and other comedy programmes.

**production values:** all the elements involved in the treatment of a production, for example, *mise en scène*, lighting, set design, quality of film/video, camera work and editing.

**product placement:** the payment by commercial companies to film-production companies of a fee for the placement of their products in key scenes and in association with celebrity actors.

- Product placement has become an important component in the financing of films.
- *e.g.* the use of Aston Martin cars in *James Bond* films

**propaganda:** media products prepared specifically to spread and reinforce a particular set of values and beliefs, without regard for any alternative position or point of view.

- Propaganda involves selection of supportive materials and the rejection of evidence that challenges the preferred view.
- *e.g.* The BBC is banned from Zimbabwe for being critical of Robert Mugabe's government.

**Propp, Vladimir (1895–1970):** Russian formalist writer and folklorist who analysed the structure of folk stories in his work *The Morphology of the Folktale* (1958).

■ His research refers to the types of character in folk tales and the events that involve them. He found that folk tales begin with an initial situation where the characters are introduced. This is followed up with 31 functions, not always present but always occurring in the same order.

■ His work emphasises the role of character in structuring narrative and is useful in helping to understand generic conventions, but it is rigid and of limited use in deconstructing complex contemporary narratives. Propp's character types include:

● the hero, character who seeks something
● the villain, who opposes the hero's quest
● the donor, who provides an object with magic property
● the dispatcher, who sends the hero on his way with a message
● the false hero, who disrupts the hero's hope of reward by making false claims
● the helper, who aids the hero
● the princess, the reward for the hero and an object of the villain's scheming
● her father, who rewards the hero for his efforts

■ *TIP* Do not attempt to force narratives into Propp's structure. It is enough to remember that he focuses on character and the generic conventions of folk tales and argues for the similarity of structure behind all narratives. Contemporary narrative, while working within expectations and conventions, often subverts the expectations of audiences rather than offering them comfortable and predictable characters and outcomes.

**protagonist:** the leading character or hero in a film with whom the audience can identify and from whose point of view the action is positioned, often set in binary opposition against the antagonist.

**PSB:** see public service broadcasting.

**public interest:** the claim that general public concern and the 'need to know' provide justification for a type of media coverage of behaviour and events which might otherwise be seen as intrusive and invasive of the privacy of individuals or organisations.

■ *e.g.* The *Daily Mirror* justified publishing a photograph of model Naomi Campbell leaving a drug clinic, on the grounds that it was in the public interest to know what can happen to celebrities as a result of their lifestyle and that she actively sought publicity that reflected positively on her behaviour and enhanced her career.

**publicity:** the process of making people or events public, or of drawing public attention to them through the mass media.

■ The term is also sometimes used to mean advertising.

■ A publicist such as Max Clifford takes on the job of managing publicity for a client, usually by manipulating press coverage to create a more positive image and by suppressing negative story lines. Clifford is quoted as saying: 'The biggest part of my job is stopping stories.'

**public opinion:** the views of ordinary people as assessed by opinion polls.

■ Public opinion is a term used to describe a majority view on any issue and is seen an important indicator of **attitudes, beliefs and values** in a society. However, public opinion can be swayed and manipulated by media **representations** and **agendas**. It has therefore become an important area of study for politicians seeking election, for commercial manufacturers seeking increased sales, for advertisers seeking to persuade and for media organisations in general.

■ *Public Opinion* (1922) was an influential book by Walter **Lippmann**, who was concerned about the problem of explaining complex, modern political and economic issues in Western democracies where mass audiences are dominated by the media and powerful **elites**.

**public relations (PR):** the promotion of positive images of clients — both individuals and organisations — without drawing attention to that promotion, undertaken by specialist PR companies.

■ Public relations is a multimillion pound industry affecting all aspects of our lives. Many news stories are generated by public-relations companies seeking free publicity for clients, and government PR (**spin**) has become an accepted part of news management.

■ *e.g.* Schools and colleges do their best to have themselves positively represented in the local press with photographs, lists of examination results and interviews.

■ *TIP* Unlike advertising, public relations is meant to be invisible in the sense that audiences do not realise that what they are reading or watching has been designed to advance the positive image of an individual or organisation.

**public service broadcasting (PSB):** a philosophy of broadcasting based on the view that the broadcast media play an important role in providing a society with information, education and entertainment and that the cultural importance of this role means that broadcasting should be seen as a public service subsidised by the state rather than by a commercially based, profit-motivated enterprise. See **British Broadcasting Corporation (BBC)** and **Independent Television (ITV)**.

■ PSB is often associated with the views of Lord **Reith**, the first director general of the BBC. In Britain, the ethos has influenced government policy toward the media to the present day.

■ The terrestrial commercial ITV channels were established with a public service brief and required to provide regulated hours of drama, news and current affairs coverage in the public interest.

■ The increasingly commercial model of the deregulated broadcasting environment has left the BBC attempting to balance a public service role and the justification of its licence fee with its extensive and lucrative commercial interests.

**pyrotechnics:** the use of explosive devices in films, stage or television productions.

**qualitative research:** media research based on direct contact between the researcher and individual subjects.

■ Data are usually collected from a variety of sources, including unstructured interviews, letters and observations.

■ *TIP* A criticism of this method is that findings are often subjective in that they reflect the respondents' views of the world and are dependent on the interpretation of researchers.

**quality press:** distinguishing term applied to British broadsheet (now compact in some cases) newspapers to separate them from the popular tabloid press.

■ The quality press are seen to focus on hard news stories and responsible, balanced reporting and comment. Their readership profile shows high levels of A, B and C1 readers (see ABC1 scale) with professional and managerial roles.

**quantitative research:** media research in which a large amount of factual, objective information is gathered anonymously from a large group of viewers, readers or listeners.

■ Research methods include questionnaires and interviews. These provide information that can be presented in chart or graphic form.

■ *TIP* Critics of this method point to the lack of subjective personal context behind the statistics and are concerned that the presentational methods used in graphs, charts and tables can be devised in such a way as to distort the information provided.

**queer cinema:** a term used to describe films representing the lifestyle and experiences of gays and lesbians.

■ The term is a deliberately ironic use of the word 'queer', which is often used in a homophobic and derogatory context.

■ *e.g.* the BBC film *Oranges are Not the Only Fruit* (Beeban Kidron, 1990), an adaptation of Jeanette Winterson's novel of the same name; *Better than Chocolate* (Anne Wheeler, 2002)

**queer theory:** see Butler, Judith.

**questionnaire:** a list of standard closed questions distributed by hand or by post to a specific group of people considered appropriate to the survey.

■ Questionnaires can provide a large amount of easily assessable information.

■ Critics argue that respondents can either be intimidated by 'official' question-naires into giving the politically correct answer and concealing their true feelings or may not take them seriously, and that therefore the data are suspect. In addition, closed questions do not allow respondents to express their own thoughts since they are often forced to choose between predetermined options.

**racism:** practices and behaviour involving social and economic discrimination, based on the false assumption that one particular ethnic group or race is culturally and biologically inferior to another.

■ Racist behaviour is based on centuries of economic exploitation and has been deeply embedded in European culture. Concerns have been expressed about the role played by the media in sustaining and reinforcing race stereotypes.

■ Stuart Hall first raised concerns about negative representations of black people on British television in 1971 and has since (1995) investigated representations of black people in period films, identifying three types: faithful happy slaves, primitive and cunning natives and clowns or entertainers. Hall sees such negative stereotypes as reinforcing **dominant ideology** by making slavery and colonialism appear acceptable and by inviting black people themselves to accept the **hegemonic** position e.g. *Gone with the Wind* (Victor Fleming, 1939).

■ **Blaxploitation films** have also been accused of reinforcing negative stereotypes.

■ In spite of **multicultural** initiatives and the expansion of ethnic minority **representation** and ethnic television programming, some critics argue that racism is still institutionalised in the British media and that positive changes are token and nominal.

■ *TIP* The negative reaction of tabloid newspapers to asylum seekers could be said to have a hidden racist agenda since the majority of those seeking asylum are black or Asian.

**radical feminism:** a feminist perspective that sees men as the enemy who have used **patriarchy** and the traditional family structure to suppress all women, regardless of class, culture or ethnicity.

■ Radical feminism accuses men of denying or denigrating all female cultural achievements, and often uses extreme language to challenge aspects of male behaviour and male social practices.

■ *e.g.* Acts of sexual intercourse are seen as violence, or even rape, and representations involving female nudity are seen as 'rape fantasies' constructed for the entertainment of men, for example, Valerie Solanas (1936–88), author of the *SCUM* (Society for Cutting Up Men) *Manifesto*.

**radio:** broadcasting medium developed between 1904 and 1922 and officially established in Britain in 1927 with the founding of the **British Broadcasting Corporation** (BBC) as a broadcasting monopoly offering three radio channels.

■ Radio was the predominant medium of news, entertainment and propaganda between 1927 and 1950. It took the form of a public service in Britain but in the USA was always a commercial system carrying advertising. In Britain, radio became the focus of national identity and resistance during the Second World War.

■ In the 1930s, radio brought people from across the world (in the form of the then British Empire) together to hear the king's Christmas message.

■ Radio faced strong competition from television in the 1950s and saw declining audiences. With only three (later four) radio stations offered by the BBC and with the challenge of **pirate radio** in the early 1960s, the structure of radio broadcasting was adapted through legislation, breaking the BBC's monopoly by allowing commercial stations in 1974. Again in the 1990s, under **deregulation**, new commercial franchises encouraged the further expansion of national, local and community stations and the BBC launched Radio 5 (later changed to Radio Five Live) in 1994, with a mix of sport and lightweight news.

■ Digital radio (digital audio broadcasting or DAB), with an enhanced digital signal, has been available in the UK since 1995 and the BBC launched five digital-only services in 2002.

■ *TIP* The current trend in radio is away from centralised, national, mass audience models toward commercial, **narrowcast**, diverse, regional and ethnic stations, serving local communities and interest groups.

**Radio Authority:** the body established by the **Broadcasting Act 1990** to monitor and regulate programming and advertising on all independent (non-BBC) radio stations; replaced by **Ofcom** in 2003.

**ratings:** the viewing figures of television programmes by which their success or failure is assessed.

**razor edit:** a style of moving image editing which involves a sharp cut from one scene to another.

**reactionary:** right wing, conservative, resistant to social, political and cultural change.

**reaction shot (also known as 'nodding shot'):** a shot devised for an interview between two people, usually showing an interviewer responding to the interviewee's answers by nodding or reacting in some way.

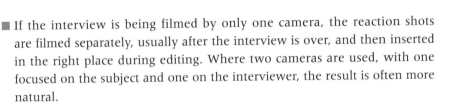

- If the interview is being filmed by only one camera, the reaction shots are filmed separately, usually after the interview is over, and then inserted in the right place during editing. Where two cameras are used, with one focused on the subject and one on the interviewer, the result is often more natural.

**readership:** the total number of people who read a publication such as a newspaper or magazine rather than just the number who buy it.

- Readership is normally estimated at between three and four times the number of copies sold (see circulation).
- The readership profile of a newspaper provides vital information for advertisers and newspaper publishers not only on the number of readers but more importantly on their social status and income, e.g. the number of young professional readers of the *Guardian*, with high levels of disposable income, makes it attractive to advertisers of consumer goods and services.
- *TIP* Newspaper readership statistics are available from the Audit Bureau of Circulation (ABC) website.

**realism:** a film and television style that attempts to represent the real world.

- Concepts of realism are governed by recognisable codes and conventions which change over time. Black and white newsreel images of the 1930s and the Second World War carried strong messages and, as filmed 'reality', defined the period in which they were constructed. Rare colour footage of the same period shocks the viewer with its sense of immediacy and newness, making the events seem fresh and the past seem just like the present.
- In the film *Schindler's List* (1993), Spielberg chose classic monochrome film and a 1930s/1940s treatment style to replicate the 'realism' of newsreels he remembered from his youth. The only colour image is of a young girl in red, a symbolic victim representing the whole holocaust.
- *TIP* Remember that film images are never 'real', they are only ever representations of the real.

**reality television:** a style of television which claims to represent real-life situations rather than scripted pre-recorded constructs, and which places members of the public in everyday or contrived situations and then films their behaviour for 'live' transmission.

- The members of the public may or may not be already known to an audience. In some instances, they might be celebrities, but their behaviour is not scripted, although games and situations may be constructed for them to respond to.
- Reality television involves exposing people to challenging encounters with others or with aspects of their own lives for the entertainment of the audience who are invited to participate in judging the participants' performance and contributions and to vote for their favourites.

■ By encouraging tensions between different participants, the television producers (backed up by newspapers) can influence how the public views their behaviour and build a simple binary narrative of heroes and villains.

■ *e.g.* *Big Brother, I'm A Celebrity…Get Me Out Of Here, The Apprentice*

**real time:** the actual viewing time of a film or video production. In computer systems the term means an instant response.

**receiver:** the actual recipient of a mass communication message (ideally but not necessarily the target audience) in a linear process model of communication.

■ *e.g.* The receivers of the messages constructed by the *Daily Mail* in any of its issues are principally the buyers of the newspaper but also anyone else who happens to read it.

**reception theory (also known as 'audience studies'):** an active audience theory, associated with the work of John Fiske, Michel de Certeau and researcher David Morley, which sees the audience as being actively engaged in the interpretation of media texts rather than as passive consumers.

■ Audiences decode media texts in ways that relate to their social and cultural circumstances and individual experience. Reception theory uses qualitative and ethnographic methods such as group interviews and participant observation.

■ In his 1980 *Nationwide* study (*Nationwide* was an evening current affairs television programme), Morley found that an audience's response to media texts was influenced by family, class and educational factors. He showed that different groups interpreted the same texts in different ways depending on their background and level of involvement with the subject matter. For example, a group of management trainees saw the programme's items on trade unions as being biased toward the unions, whereas a group of workers saw the same items as being anti-union. Morley developed the terms dominant, negotiated and oppositional readings to categorise responses.

■ Morley's approach is important because it combines semiological and sociological approaches. Semiological study involves the idea of directed preferred readings of media texts, while sociological study is concerned with how age, sex, race, class and gender may determine the reading of a text.

■ The approach is also known as audience studies or New Audience research and in the 1990s was associated with the work of David Buckingham. His research concludes that even by the age of seven children have become skilled readers of media texts and are able to interpret, challenge and reject media messages, including advertising.

■ *TIP* This research can be used to challenge effects theory models which argue that audiences, particularly children, are affected negatively by media content.

**red top:** describes a tabloid national daily newspaper that has its masthead printed on a red background.

**re-enactment:** a film or television production that attempts to reproduce actual events as accurately as possible.

■ *e.g.* *Downfall* (Oliver Hirschbiegel, 2005), the recreation of the last days of Adolf Hitler and Nazi Germany; *Iris* (Richard Eyre, 2001), the story of the tragic illness of writer Iris Murdoch

■ *TIP* Re-enactments are often incorporated into fiction narratives, for example, the D-Day landings in the opening scenes of *Saving Private Ryan* (Steven Spielberg, 1998), which were intended to convey the terrifying experience of the actual landings while being based on fictional characters. Such re-enactments add to the credibility of the fictional narrative, so blurring the distinction between fiction and reality in the eyes of the audience.

**register:** the style and tone of language used in a printed media text.

■ Register includes grammatical features, the choice of vocabulary and the mode of address adopted by a publication, which together structure the discourse being established with the reader.

■ *e.g.* The *Sun*, *The Times*, *The Economist*, *Loaded*, *Nuts*, *Computer Weekly* and the *New Law Journal* all have different readerships and different registers.

**Registrar General's social scale:** the system for classifying the population by social class and occupation, used at times of national census.

■ A version of the scale used by advertisers and market researchers is known as the ABC1 scale.

**Reith, John (1889–1971):** first general manager of the British Broadcasting Company at its founding in 1922 and later first director general of the British Broadcasting Corporation (BBC), 1927–38.

■ Under Reith, the BBC developed a distinctive style and purpose and became a highly conservative institution and supporter of the establishment. However, Reith was also determined to maintain the BBC's independence from direct government interference and established its worldwide reputation for quality of programming and objectivity of news reporting.

■ Reith's public service vision of the BBC was partly dependent on its monopoly of broadcasting and was challenged by the advent of independent commercial television. However, his vision remained the dominant ethos of broadcasting in the UK until deregulation in 1990.

**remake:** a new version of a previously successful film that closely follows the original but adapts it in line with changing audience expectations.

■ The popularity of remakes, involving the use of financially safe, tried and tested formulas, is often cited in criticisms of mainstream Hollywood production companies for their lack of originality and unwillingness to take risks.

■ *e.g. The Italian Job* (Peter Collinson, 1969), remake *The Italian Job* (F. Gary Gray, 2003); *Cape Fear* (J. Lee Thompson, 1962), remake *Cape Fear* (Martin Scorsese, 1991)

**representation:** `key concept` the process whereby the media construct versions of people, places and events in images, words or sound for transmission through media texts to an audience.

■ Representations provide models of how we see gender, social groups, individuals and aspects of the world we all inhabit. They are ideological in that they are constructed within a framework of values and beliefs. Representations are therefore **mediated** and reflect the value systems of their sources. No representation is ever real, only a version of the real.

■ Representations are part of cultural mythology and reflect deep-seated values and beliefs, e.g. of such places as the north of England, Scotland and America.

■ *TIP* Representation is the key to many media debates and is usually described as being positive or negative, depending on the view of the group being represented. Achieving positive representations (versions of themselves that they agree with and approve of) has been a goal of minority groups who have criticised the perceived negativity of media **stereotypes**, e.g. gays, ethnic minorities, religious minorities, disability groups and women.

**research:** the process of identifying and compiling data or evidence for investigation into an aspect of the media under study.

■ When considering research areas, it is always important to consider the outcomes that are to be achieved and to apply research to the specific question under study.

■ **Primary research** is conducted at first-hand through surveys, interviews, personal **content analysis** exercises etc. It involves the logging and recording of findings and can produce large amounts of **qualitative** data. This is often demanding and difficult but makes work distinctive.

■ **Secondary research** involves investigating information gathered by others from books, pamphlets, radio, television and magazines. The majority of research is likely to be of this type.

■ *TIP* In your own research, try to make a comparison between similar media texts rather than concentrating on just one, and try to show a broad awareness of the history and development of the subject under study. You should also relate your study to appropriate theory and to the **key concept**.

**resolution (1):** the conclusion of a **narrative** in such a way that all outstanding problems, questions and uncertainties are solved, answered or clarified to the satisfaction of the audience.

**resolution (2):** the quality of an image, measured in horizontal and vertical **pixels**.

■ The higher the resolution, the better the quality of the image. A high-resolution digital camera has 1920 × 1600 pixels while a low-resolution one has 640 × 480 pixels. High-resolution digital images produce larger files and take up more computer storage space, but they have much better picture quality. A film has high resolution when it has a slow ASA speed and a fine grain.

**Reuters:** the largest international multimedia news agency, providing news and financial information to the media, corporates and individuals, with employees in 92 countries.

■ Reuters has a 20% stake in the ownership of Independent Television News.

**right-wing:** having conservative or fascist political leanings; being supportive of the status quo and dominant ideology in a society, together with traditional family values and minimum social change.

**road movie:** a film genre in which the leading characters embark on a journey or quest, often in search of an ideal, and encounter a range of people and situations on their way.

■ Road movies can often involve sentimental or romantic interpretations of the American Dream, e.g. *The Wizard of Oz* (Victor Fleming, 1939).

■ *e.g. Easy Rider* (Dennis Hopper, 1969), *Wild at Heart* (David Lynch, 1990), *Thelma and Louise* (Ridley Scott, 1991)

**Rolling Stone:** music magazine, founded as a 24-page music newspaper by Jann Wenner in 1967 and published by Wenner Publishing.

■ *Rolling Stone* is the classic music magazine. From its foundation as the cornerstone of 1960s rock counterculture, it has changed its format to becoming a celebrity-fronted music and gossip magazine, but still carries serious reviews and political and cultural commentaries.

■ *TIP* Many see *Rolling Stone* as a throwback to the 1960s and less in touch with the contemporary music scene than such publications as *NME*, the music and entertainment magazine *Word* and the rock magazine *Kerrang*.

**romantic comedy:** a film genre developed in 1930s Hollywood where the two main protagonists are a man and a woman who seem to be at odds with each other but end up romantically involved.

■ The genre was associated in the 1930s with such stars as Cary Grant and Katharine Hepburn and more recently, in its Brit Film version, with Hugh Grant in such films as *Notting Hill* (Roger Michell, 1999) and *Love Actually* (Richard Curtis, 2003).

**rushes:** the daily footage of a film, viewed unedited straight from the camera.

**satellite phone:** a technological development in which a mobile phone is linked to a communications satellite so that a visual as well as an audio message can be transmitted.

■ Satellite telephones are often used where normal communication is difficult, for example, in disaster zones, war zones and remote areas. Although picture quality is often poor and the signal may break up, the images enhance the sense of immediacy and involvement for the viewer.

**satire:** mocking, scornful humour, heavily dependent on sarcasm, irony and wit.

■ In a modern sense, political satire is a form of comedy that ridicules politicians and other figures in the public eye by exposing their follies and the contradictions inherent in their behaviour and public pronouncements.

■ *e.g.* magazine: *Private Eye* (1960s–); television: *Spitting Image* (1980s) and *Bremner Bird and Fortune* (1990s–)

**Saussure, Ferdinand de (1857–1913):** a linguist, often styled 'the father of semiology', who devised a system of analysing language using deconstruction methods rather than traditional grammar.

■ His approach saw language as a symbolic sign system in which elements from categories (paradigms) are combined in such a way as to create meaningful utterances (syntagms). The rules of these combinations depend on the codes being used and the possible combinations allowed in any particular language.

■ Saussure's work has inspired not only linguists but also those analysing images of the new visual media. Roland Barthes, in particular, developed semiology by applying Saussure's ideas to film, television, magazines and popular culture.

**schedule:** the running order of television and radio programmes.

**scheduling:** the practice of placing programmes on radio and television in such a way as to meet the expectations of particular audiences and to maximise viewing and listening figures.

**Schramm, Wilbur (1907–87):** US researcher responsible for producing an influential **process model** of mass communication (1954), which isolated **encoding** and **decoding** processes, allowed for **feedback** from an audience and divided the mass audience into network groups, where some members were seen as more influential in passing on media messages than others.

■ His approach challenged the uniform 'mass' audience concept and led to the later development of the idea of **opinion leaders** and **two-step flow** theory.

**science fiction:** a film genre involving a futuristic or alien world setting, and technologies not available in the contemporary world.

■ The first film in the genre was *Metropolis* (Fritz Lang, 1927). The futuristic writings of H. G. Wells provided screenplays for *Things to Come* (William Cameron Menzies, 1936) and *The War of the Worlds* (Byron Haskin, 1954) and its remake, *War of the Worlds* (Steven Spielberg, 2005).

■ The imaginary future often has a **dystopian** setting or reflects current fears and phobias such as alien or foreign invasion (*Independence Day*, Roland Emmerich, 1996), technological nightmares (*The Terminator*, James Cameron, 1984), or ecological disaster (*Waterworld*, Kevin Reynolds, 1995). The genre is equally adaptable to the mystical and mysterious (*2001: A Space Odyssey*, Stanley Kubrick, 1968) and to fairy-tale fantasy narrative (*Star Wars*, George Lucas, 1977) and horror (*Alien*, Ridley Scott, 1979).

■ See **cyberpunk**

**scopophilia:** a term used by the psychologist Sigmund Freud to describe 'the pleasure of looking'.

■ The term is used by Laura **Mulvey** in the development of her **'male gaze'** theory in her essay *Visual Pleasure and Narrative Cinema* (1975).

**screenplay:** the script of a film production, including dialogue, lighting, camerawork and setting, used by the director during filming (see **shooting script**).

**screen time:** the duration of a television programme which, in the case of a dramatic narrative, is usually shorter than the narrative's **story time** covered during the programme.

■ *e.g.* The screentime of an average soap opera episode is around half an hour, but usually represents one or more days of story time.

**search engine:** computer software that scans the **internet** in response to selected words or phrases and then lists website findings for users to choose from.

■ *e.g. Google, Yahoo*

**secondary research:** research that involves using the work of others, including books, magazines, websites and published articles.

■ The majority of background research undertaken for a media project or essay will be secondary research, but your own analysis of a media text is classed as primary research.

**segmentation:** the concentration by individual satellite and cable television channels on one area of viewing, such as sport, film, history, shopping, religion and science fiction.

■ *e.g.* CBeebies, Nick TV, Fox Kids, The Disney Channel

**self-regulation:** the use of voluntary codes of practice, devised by the advertising, television and newspaper industries as a means of policing their own performance and behaviour, with the aim of avoiding what they see as restrictive government legislation.

■ The control of the press is a particularly sensitive area because of the principle of a 'free press' in a pluralist democracy. Some would argue, however, that the press often abuse this freedom in pursuit of sensational celebrity-led stories, and that the regulatory body lacks sufficient powers to protect the rights of the individual to privacy (see Press Complaints Commission, Advertising Standards Authority, Ofcom).

**semiology (also known as 'semiotics'):** the study of signs.

■ Semiology provides a system for deconstructing and analysing visual and moving images and for explaining the wider cultural choice and combination patterns that generate cultural meaning.

■ Semiology takes its name from *sēmeion*, the Greek word for sign, and assumes that all communication codes are arbitrary and that there is no logical reason why we use a particular sign. Meaning is seen as deriving from the creator of the sign, the reader of the sign and the nature of the sign itself.

**sender:** the initiator of a mass-communication message in a linear process model of communication.

■ *e.g.* A broadcasting organisation is the initiator or 'sender' of a television news programme.

**sequel:** a follow-up production to a successful film release, often planned as part of the overall project.

■ *e.g.* The *Terminator* movies were planned to allow for sequels to the original.

**serial:** a television or radio narrative that presents daily or weekly episodes, with multiple sets of recurring characters and parallel story lines, where each episode links to the next and closure is rare.

■ *e.g.* A soap opera is a continuing serial without an end.

**series:** a television or radio narrative that presents self-contained weekly episodes, using a recurring set of characters.

■ *e.g.* *Friends* (1994–2004).

**server:** a computer that provides an information service to other computers linked to it through a network.

■ On the World Wide Web, the term can also refer to a program that responds to requests for web pages from a browser.

**service provider:** see internet service provider.

**set:** the constructed environment in which a film is placed and shot.

**sexism:** representations that discriminate on the basis of sex, especially against women, which is seen to derive from and sustain patriarchy.

■ Some feminists would see any media representation of women that confirmed a stereotype as sexist, for example, the display of women's bodies as sex objects in lads mags for the entertainment of men.

■ *TIP* In a post-feminist environment, challenges are launched at representations of men that show them as sex objects or as being humiliated at the hands of women.

**SFX:** a broad term often used on a storyboard, meaning sound or special effects.

**Shannon, Claude (1916–2001) and Weaver, Warren (1894–1978):** researchers responsible for producing an influential linear process model of communication in 1949.

**shooting script:** a written description, shot by shot, of a film or television programme, detailing the sequence, location and type of camera shot making up the production and used by the cast and crew during the 'shoot' (see screenplay).

***Sight and Sound:*** monthly magazine of the British Film Institute, dedicated to the visual image and containing detailed reviews of most major film releases.

■ *TIP Sight and Sound* reviews are good examples of quality film writing, consisting of a detailed cast and production team list, a film plot synopsis and a personal critique of the film.

**sign:** a term introduced by Saussure to describe the combination of the signifier and the signified, where the signifier is the physical object and the signified is the mental concept or meaning that the signifier conveys.

■ A photograph of a rose makes the viewer think of the flower.

■ Pierce developed different categories of the sign to explain the relationship with what he described as their object.

**signifier:** the physical object used to represent a mental concept.

■ *e.g.* The word 'tree' represents the physical object, the tree, as an idea in the mind of the reader. The Eiffel Tower signifies, or represents, the idea of Paris.

**silent film:** a film produced between 1900 and 1927 without a recorded soundtrack.

■ Before film technology developed to the extent where a soundtrack could be scored alongside the running film, all sound was added separately to film and either provided by instruments, whole orchestras or accompanying discs which had to be effectively synchronised with the screen action.

■ The term does not mean that such performances were 'silent', only that the sound was an additional extra.

■ The development of a scored soundtrack (the first sound film was *The Jazz Singer*, Alan Crosland, 1927) allowed the voices of actors to be recorded alongside the action, but also had constraining effects in that the action had to be studio-based and within reach of primitive microphones.

■ *TIP* Do not underestimate the cinematic freedom and variety accorded to silent film, which was not constrained by primitive studio-based sound-recording facilities and was therefore free to range outdoors, e.g. *Nosferatu* (F. W. Murnau, 1922), *Napoleon* (Abel Gance, 1927).

**silent majority:** a term used by politicians to invent a consensus of support for their views ostensibly from a section of the population who remain silent during media debates on policy and values.

■ The politician as opinion leader claims to access the thoughts of those who say nothing and attaches them to his or her own cause. The silent majority is usually invoked in support of mainstream, dominant ideology and the status quo.

**simulacrum (plural simulacra):** any stage in the relationship between the real world and its representation where the distinction between reality and its image, between signs and what they refer to, has been progressively broken down.

■ The term was first used by the French postmodernist critic Jean Baudrillard.

■ Reality becomes redundant when hyperreality — more real than real — and the mingling and self-generation of images without reference to reality or meaning takes over consciousness.

■ The postmodern world is one of computer-generated fantasy characters being replicated by real people (e.g. Lara Croft in the *Tomb Raider* games and films) and of virtual and simulated experience replacing actual experience.

**situation comedy:** a television or radio comedy in which characters are located in a particular contained environment which forms the basis of their relationships and the centre of the action.

■ This can be a workplace (*Are You being Served?*), a domestic setting (*Rising Damp, Terry and June, Absolutely Fabulous*), a prison (*Porridge*), a space ship (*Red Dwarf*) or any other restricted location.

**Sky:** see British Sky Broadcasting.

**Sky Digital:** British Sky Broadcasting's digital satellite holdings, offering the widest choice of digital channels in the UK.

**slasher movie:** a subgenre of the horror film, where horror is generated by murders committed with a knife.

■ Slasher films usually focus on a group of teenagers who are pursued and murdered one by one, until only one character remains. This is often the 'final girl' who identifies and kills the murderer.

■ The genre is directed at teenagers and usually carries moral messages about punishment for sexual promiscuity, where only 'good' girls (i.e. virgins) are spared the killer's knife.

■ *e.g.* *Psycho* (Alfred Hitchcock, 1960) is often cited as the first slasher movie but the origin of the genre is more often associated with *Halloween* (John Carpenter, 1978). More recently, parodies of the genre appeared with *Scream* (Wes Craven, 1996), *Cherry Falls* (Geoffrey Wright, 2000) and *Scary Movie* (Keenan Ivory Wayans, 2000).

**soap opera:** a continuous, episodic serial on radio or television based on community life.

■ Originating from US radio series of the 1930s that were sponsored by a soap powder company, 'soaps' have grown to become one of the most popular television forms worldwide.

■ Extensive studies have been done on the nature of soap operas, including their use of realism or fantasy, character representation, audience appeal and scriptwriting techniques. They are seen as addictive by their many viewers, but the pressure of sustaining story lines can render scripts and characters increasingly unrealistic.

■ In Britain, soaps guarantee a regular audience and are increasingly used for this purpose by rival television channels. For example, the Channel 4 teen-soap *Hollyoaks* expanded from twice weekly showings to being scheduled five nights a week to help secure an early evening audience.

■ *TIP* Not all soap operas are launched successfully. The British Broadcasting Corporation lost large sums of money with the failed soap *Eldorado* (1992–93), based in the fictional Spanish holiday resort of Los Barcos.

**social action broadcasting:** television and radio programming which is designed both to analyse current social problems and issues and to encourage people to respond to what they have seen and heard.

■ Social action programmes are a form of interactive television and radio.

■ *e.g.* *Crimewatch UK*

**social realism:** the representation of characters and issues in film and television drama in such a way as to raise serious underlying social and political issues.

■ Social realism involves a drama–documentary treatment in the sense that, while the characters may be fictional, the contexts and circumstances in which they are placed represent existing social realities.

■ The films are usually shot in a naturalistic way, avoiding the use of sophisticated editing and treatments and sometimes giving the impression that the camera is simply recording events as they take place. There is often little use of non-diegetic sound.

■ *e.g.* the films of British director Ken Loach, *Kes* (1970) and *Sweet Sixteen* (2002)

**soft focus:** in images, the use of a special lense or filter to create a hazy light around the subject.

■ Soft focus shots are associated with a romantic or sentimental treatment of subject matter.

**soft news:** news involving human interest rather than political or economic content.

■ Soft news is seen as populist and is often associated with dumbing down.

**Sony:** vertically integrated, multimedia global corporation with headquarters in Culver City, California, USA.

■ Sony has wide media interests, including film production via Columbia Pictures, multiplex cinema operation through Loews Cineplex Entertainment, and the production of media-related consumer goods including DVD recorders and televisions.

**sound bite:** a short phrase inserted into the speeches of politicians by their speech writers to provide a memorable summary of a policy statement or viewpoint. Sound bites make good headlines and also fit well in television and radio news programmes.

■ *e.g.* Tony Blair in the 1997 election: 'Education, Education, Education', using the so-called 'rule of three' to emphasise New Labour's commitment to improving the education system. John F. Kennedy in the 1960 US presidential inauguration speech used a neat and memorable circular phrase to make his point: 'Ask not what your country can do for you but what you can do for your country.'

**sound effects:** enhanced sound added to a film or television programme during postproduction.

■ Sound effects are designed to complement the visual content of a film and heighten the audience's experience.

■ In horror or gangster films, melons slashed with knives are often used to represent the sound of a body being stabbed.

**spaghetti Western:** a genre variation of the Western developed during the 1960s and 1970s.

S

■ Spaghetti Westerns were filmed in Spain and Italy and closely associated with the Italian director Sergio Leone and the actor Clint Eastwood as 'the man with no name'. They have an exaggerated and melodramatic style, using overdrawn stock characters, limited dialogue and heavily staged 'shoot-out' confrontations.

■ *e.g. Fistful of Dollars* (Sergio Leone, 1964), *The Good, the Bad and the Ugly* (Sergio Leone, 1966)

**spike:** journalistic term for the rejection of a story, originating in the practice of sticking 'dead' stories onto a metal spike.

**spin:** manipulated information offered to journalists by press officers and communication managers who aim to ensure that their employers are favourably represented.

■ The term is usually used in a political context but is also present in the commercial world. In the context of newspapers and journalism, spin is the angle or point of view adopted within any particular story.

**spin doctor:** a public relations or press officer charged with manipulating information released to the press in order to ensure that issues are represented in ways favourable to their employer.

■ In politics, the term also describes those whose role it is to attempt to manipulate the political **agenda** on behalf of government and ensure that issues are debated on the government's terms.

■ *e.g.* In an e-mail leaked to the press, a communications manager for the British government (Jo Moore) told a colleague that 11 September 2001 was 'a good day to bury bad news'. What she meant was that because all attention was focused on the destruction of the twin towers, people would not notice other news reports and the government could therefore release unfavourable statistics or details of unpopular decisions without their being noticed.

**spiral of silence:** model of **public opinion** formation devised by Elizabeth Noelle-Neumann in 1974, which examined the reasons why minority opinion in a society can go unheard.

■ The model is based on the assumption that people feel uneasy if they find themselves isolated in relation to general opinion around them. If they feel that they hold a minority view on a topic, increasingly they will find it difficult to express their opinion in public. The dominant view will thus appear even more dominant because those who disagree with it remain silent.

■ To overcome the uncomfortable feeling of being out of line, individuals may change their opinion in order to feel part of the majority.

■ *e.g.* Membership of the Nazi Party in Germany increased after Hitler came to power (see **hegemony**).

**split screen:** an editing technique which involves the cinema screen being split into two or more parts to allow the showing of events that are taking place at the same time.

■ Split-screen editing has been used since the earliest films, e.g. *Napoleon* (Abel Gance, 1927) used a triple-screen split.

■ *e.g.* *Run Lola Run* (Tom Tykwer, 1998)

**sponsorship:** a business relationship whereby a company provides funding for an individual, project, event (or, in radio and television, a programme) in return for a commercial benefit, usually in terms of advertising time or space.

**spoof:** a light-hearted, humorous text that parodies a known text or theme.

■ *e.g.* *Scream* (Wes Craven, 1996), a spoof horror; *Without a Clue* (Thom Eberhardt, 1988), a spoof Sherlock Holmes detective story

**spot colour:** in advertising, the addition of spots (small patches), usually of one colour, to a black and white advertisement.

**SR theory:** see stimulus response theory.

**stake-out:** a news report in which the reporter addresses his or her commentary directly to the camera.

**stand-up:** part of a television news package in which the reporter stands in front of a site significant to the events he or she is describing.

***Star*:** a tabloid red top newspaper, owned by Express Newspapers and originally launched to target young male readers with a diet of sport, sex and gossip.

■ The paper shows an indifference to politics and world affairs.

■ Although lower in circulation than the other tabloid newspapers (861,000 copies, January 2005), the *Star* has broadened its efforts to attract readers by adopting a celebrity-based, broad entertainment approach to news.

**star system:** the practice of constructing a film around a particular successful actor in order to secure box-office success.

■ The use of well-known stars in association with particular film genres was a part of the Hollywood studio system of the 1930s and 1940s, e.g. Cary Grant and romantic comedy.

■ Contemporary films are still structured around stars, e.g. the *Terminator* series with Arnold Schwarzenegger, and Richard Curtis's romantic comedies starring Hugh Grant — *Four Weddings and a Funeral* (1994), *Notting Hill* (1998) and *Love Actually* (2003).

■ See A-list.

**status quo:** leaving things as they are.

■ Mainstream media representations tend to support a status quo view of human life, particularly with regard to socioeconomic power structures and many aspects of cultural behaviour.

**steadycam:** a portable camera strapped to a cameraman with a harness to produce a smooth floating image of the subject.

■ Steadycams provide an alternative to the hand-held camera's crude wobbling effect and can make the viewer feel that he or she is floating through the action and around the characters.

■ Steadycams are often used for point-of-view shots and are also used extensively in sports coverage.

**stereotype:** the social classification of a group of people by identifying common characteristics and universally applying them in an often oversimplified and generalised way, such that the classification represents value judgements and assumptions about the group concerned.

■ *e.g.* the 'dumb' blonde, the 'mean' Yorkshireman

**stimulus response theory (also known as 'SR theory'):** a term taken from behaviourist psychology, used in support of the argument that audiences respond directly to the stimuli in media texts.

■ SR theory is associated with passive audience theory, in particular the hypodermic model, which views a media message as a drug administered to a passive audience with immediate behavioural effects.

■ Some researchers still apply the stimulus response theory, e.g. with copy cat crimes, video nasties and the Jamie Bulger case.

■ *TIP* This approach is no longer seen as an adequate method of exploring the complexities of individual reactions to media texts.

**stock character:** a stereotypical, predictable minor character.

■ *e.g.* the storekeeper or bartender in a Western

**stop-motion:** a special effect achieved by filming of puppets or clay models one frame at a time, with slight repositioning to create the impression of movement.

■ The technique has been used with clay models to create moving dinosaurs, mythical beasts, and space monsters.

■ *e.g.* *King Kong* (Ernest Schoedsack, 1933), *It Came from Beneath the Sea* (Robert Gordon, 1955), *Clash of the Titans* (Desmond Davis, 1981) and *Chicken Run* (Peter Lord and Nick Park, 2000), and also television productions such as *Bob the Builder*

**storyboard:** a sequence of drawings, with accompanying camera and lighting instructions and location, dialogue and sound details, which explain how and where a scene is to be filmed.

■ A storyboard is an essential part of the initial film production process and allows for effective planning of every shot.

■ *TIP* Whether or not a storyboard is a requirement of a practical film-production brief, one should be prepared since it enables planning for the shoot to proceed more smoothly.

**story time:** the time represented in the narrative of a piece of television, film or radio drama, usually a much longer period than the screen time taken up by broadcasting or showing the production.

**straight-to-video:** a film that fails to achieve cinema distribution for financial or aesthetic reasons and is therefore only available on video or digital versatile (video) disk.

■ *TIP* A straight-to-video usually indicates commercial or artistic failure but can be a marketing strategy, particularly for independent producers who cannot find a distributor for their work.

**strand:** in television, a collection of unrelated programmes in the same genre grouped together under a generic title.

■ *e.g.* documentaries, history, science, the arts

■ *TIP* A programme strand is not the same thing as a series where all programmes are related.

**stranding:** the practice of scheduling a television programme in the same genre at the same time, each day of the week, every week.

■ *e.g.* the History Zone

**structuralism:** an intellectual movement originating in the 1960s, associated with a number of French writers and characterised by a study of the systems, relations and forms — the structures — that make meaning possible in any cultural activity or text.

■ A basic assumption of structuralism is that there are universal structures underlying different human cultures and texts.

■ The methodology has been applied to literature, language, film, fine art, psychology, anthropology, history and philosophy. Structuralism relies heavily on the terminology developed by semiologists such as Saussure and Barthes.

■ *TIP* Key names in structuralism:
Ferdinand de Saussure: semiology (originator of the system)
Roland Barthes: culture and media
Claude Levi-Strauss: anthropology and narrative
Michel Foucault: history and philosophy
Jacques Lacan: psychology and philosophy
Jacques Derrida: language
Do not confuse this with the structuralism of sociologists. This would most likely be concerned with the social structure and its part in shaping behaviour through the social organisation of society, e.g. structures such as the family, schools, religion etc. and their effects on social life.

**studio system:** the semi-industrial process of film manufacturing which was dominated by large studios during the golden age in Hollywood from the early 1930s until 1948.

S

■ The system was dominated by five studios — Warner Brothers, Twentieth Century Fox, RKO (RKO Radio Pictures), Metro-Goldwyn-Mayer and Paramount — who controlled all aspects of production, including the stars, as well as owning cinemas and ensuring worldwide distribution of their films.

**sub-editor (also known as 'sub'):** the person on a newspaper responsible for checking, rewriting and adapting stories to fit available space.

■ The sub-editor also provides captions and headlines and has some gatekeeping and spin control.

**subgenre:** a film genre that exists within a larger genre.

■ *e.g.* Slasher and vampire are subgenres within the broader horror genre.

**subjective:** from the subject's point of view.

■ A subjective response or opinion is one that is based on an individual's attitudes, beliefs and values rather than on any objective detached criteria: in tabloid terms, a 'gut reaction'.

■ According to semiologists, by consuming media texts, individuals are seen as bringing their own subjective experience to the construction of meaning, which is therefore both culturally determined and individually adjusted in line with each person's unique experience.

**subjective shot:** a type of shot in which the camera is positioned as if looking at the world through the subject's eyes.

■ *e.g.* The opening title sequence of *Taxi Driver* (Martin Scorsese, 1976) shows the world through the eyes of driver Travis Bickle (Robert DeNiro) as he views the streets through the rain on his windscreen. The image is blurred and distorted, as is his view of the world.

**subliminal advertising:** a form of advertising that works on a subconscious level by introducing barely perceptible messages into other media texts and therefore influencing consumers without their realising it.

■ *e.g.* In 1990 the Pepsi Cola Company was forced to withdraw a 'Cool Can' design because when the cans were stacked in six-packs the word 'SEX' emerged from the design. During the 2000 presidential election campaign in the USA, a Republican television advertisement criticising the Democrats flashed the word 'RATS' across the screen when describing their policies.

**subversive:** undermining of dominant ideology and values.

■ Challenging media texts are called subversive, particularly by those who see the media as a threat to mainstream values.

■ *e.g.* By challenging US attitudes to the ownership and use of guns, the film *Bowling for Columbine* (Michael Moore, 2002) subverts the dominant view that gun ownership is a natural part of the US way of life.

**Sun:** a popular tabloid newspaper, part of News International, owned by Rupert Murdoch.

■ Acquired by Murdoch in 1969, the *Sun* challenged the then most popular paper, the *Daily Mirror*, overtaking the latter's circulation in 1978 and becoming a national institution, with a daily sale of over 4 million. Its style combined eye-grabbing headlines, page 3 topless models, sex and scandal, soap operas, sport and celebrity gossip and right-wing, anti-European politics.

■ During the 1980s and early 1990s, the paper claimed to have won election victories for the Conservatives and continued supporting the party until 1997, when it switched to New Labour. Cultivating the support of the *Sun* has become an important feature of political parties seeking election success and it has helped to encourage the tabloidisation and dumbing down of British politics.

■ In 2003, the *Sun* became the first tabloid daily to appoint a female editor when Rebecca Wade took the job.

■ Its circulation figures are now down in line with other tabloid publications and stand at 3,382,000 (January 2005).

■ *TIP* Sun headlines to remember:

*Freddie Star Ate My Hamster*

*Gotcha* — on the sinking of an Argentine warship by a British submarine in the Falklands War 1982

*Hop off you Frogs* — directed against the French and the European Union

*If Kinnock wins today will the last person in Britain please turn out the lights* — an anti-Labour party header on the day of the 1992 election, with the then Labour leader Kinnock's head photo-montaged as a light bulb

*It's the Sun Wot Won It!* — the paper's verdict on the 1992 Conservative election victory; repeated, with a variation, after the 1997 New Labour victory, with the words *It's the Sun Wot Swung It*, when the *Sun* had transferred its support to New Labour

**Sunday Express:** a tabloid Sunday newspaper with right-wing positioning, owned by Richard Desmond's Express Newspapers (circulation 976,055 copies, January 2005).

■ The paper was once seen as a rival to the *Mail on Sunday* but is now so far behind in circulation as to present no real challenge.

**Sunday Mirror:** a left-of-centre tabloid Sunday newspaper, owned by Mirror Group Newspapers as part of the Trinity Mirror group (circulation 1,652,375 copies, January 2005).

**Sunday People:** a left-of-centre tabloid Sunday newspaper owned by Mirror Group Newspapers as part of the Trinity Mirror group.

■ With a circulation well below its sister paper the *Sunday Mirror*, the *Sunday People* is steadily loosing ground (circulation 1,001,389 copies, January 2005).

**Sunday Telegraph:** a Conservative-supporting, quality, broadsheet Sunday newspaper, owned by the *Daily Telegraph* (circulation 692,107 copies, January 2005).

**Sunday Times, The:** the largest circulation, quality, broadsheet Sunday newspaper, owned by News International (circulation 1,375,382 copies, January 2005).

■ *The Sunday Times* is a Conservative-supporting newspaper in principle, but in line with other News International publications tends to support the policies of New Labour.

**surrealism:** a highly influential twentieth-century art movement that emphasises the importance of the subconscious in art, founded by André Breton in 1924.

■ Key figures in the original movement include the painters Salvador Dali and Max Ernst, the photographer Man Ray and the Spanish film director Luis Buñuel.

■ Influenced by the work of Sigmund Freud on dreams and the subconscious, surrealist films have non-linear, dreamlike narratives, with episodic elements and fragmented dialogue, ambiguous characters, dreamlike settings and experimental camera work.

■ *e.g.* Dali and Buñuel received shock reactions for their films *Un Chien Andalou* (1929) and *L'Âge d'Or* (1930). Dali provided sets taken from imagery in his paintings in *Spellbound* (Alfred Hitchcock, 1945). US director David Lynch is influenced by surrealism, e.g. *Eraserhead* (1977), *Blue Velvet* (1986), *Twin Peaks: Fire Walk with Me* (1992), *Lost Highway* (1997) and *Mulholland Drive* (2001).

**surround sound:** a sound system designed to create the impression of multi-directional sound in a cinema or home-entertainment environment.

■ In the cinema, the impression of being totally immersed in the sound effects from a film enhances the overall viewing experience and creates a sense of total involvement in the action.

**suspense:** in a film and television audience, the creation of a feeling of tension and anticipation.

■ Suspense involves information concerning characters or outcomes of a film being concealed from an audience to generate feelings of excitement and surprise.

**suspension of disbelief:** the way in which an audience accepts the artificial world of the stage, film or television as real for the duration of a performance.

■ Members of the audience know that what they are watching is only a fictional construction but, in order to feel total engagement and gain maximum enjoyment, they allow their imaginations to take over and accept what is put before them as 'real'.

■ *TIP* Take care when you use this phrase. It is 'suspension of disbelief' not 'suspension of belief'.

**sweetening:** a postproduction process whereby a sound technician adds more sound effects, for example applause and laughter, to those that may already be provided by the studio audience.

■ *TIP* Postproduction-added or canned laughter can cue the television viewing audience's responses and sometimes make a programme seem more entertaining than it really is. It is interesting, for example, to view an episode of *Friends* while ignoring the laughter and to consider what is really so funny about the scene and dialogue.

**sword and sandals:** a film genre set in the ancient or biblical world.

■ Sword and sandals films began in the earliest days of cinema in Italy and were then developed in Hollywood. They are re-creations of the ancient Mediterranean, often Roman, past, using classical texts and historical figures as their basis. Sets are lavish, involving the reconstruction of classical cities and buildings, and themes involve war, passion, religion and natural disaster. Many 'sword and sandals' movies are set in the time of Christ.

■ The genre had become unfashionable until the success of *Gladiator* (Ridley Scott, 2000), after which a new generation of ancient world movies with computer-generated imagery appeared.

■ *e.g.* *Ultimi Giorni di Pompeii — The Last Days of Pompeii* (Luighi Maggi, 1908), *Quo Vadis* (Mervyn LeRoy, 1951), *The Robe* (Henry Koster, 1953), *Ben-Hur* (William Wyler, 1959), *Spartacus* (Stanley Kubrick, 1960), *Cleopatra* (Joseph Mankiewicz, 1963), *Gladiator* (Ridley Scott, 2000), *Alexander* (Oliver Stone, 2004) and *Troy* (Wolfgang Peterson, 2004)

**symbiosis:** a mutually beneficial partnership between organisations of different types, especially where one lives or is contained within the other.

■ In media industries, the term can be used to describe the situation in which subdivisions of large media companies specialising in different areas of media production work to each other's advantage.

■ *e.g.* BskyB and the *Sun* are both part of Rupert Murdoch's **News Corporation** and the *Sun* constantly advertises and provides a free platform for BSkyB products in the newspaper.

**symbol:** a sign that bears no obvious visual relation to what it represents.

■ *e.g.* the Mercedes Benz three-point star

**synchronic:** in narrative, describing events taking place at the same time.

■ Synchronic is the opposite of **diachronic** which means moving through time sequentially.

■ *e.g.* During a triple-split screen sequence in *Run Lola Run* (Tom Tykwer, 1998), we see Lola running towards, and her boyfriend Mani walking away from, a meeting point, while crucially a clock shows time passing. The scene is one of great tension.

S

**synergy:** the coming together of two separate media texts in such a way as to benefit both.

■ Synergy usually means that the combination of elements has a greater effect than the individual elements would have alone. With media texts, for example, this can mean that the simultaneous release of a film and a film sound track will stimulate greater consumer interest than if the products had been released separately.

■ *e.g.* The film *Titanic* (James Cameron, 1997) included the Oscar-winning song 'My Heart Will Go On' by Celine Dion, released as a single from the album *Let's Talk About Love*, which sold 23 million copies worldwide.

**syntagm:** any combination of signs that forms an ordered chain of meaning, for example, a sentence of written language, a strip cartoon, a narrative film or the various elements of a poster when read together as having one meaning.

■ The term was first devised by Saussure and developed by Barthes in his work *Elements of Semiology* (1964).

**tabloid:** a newspaper of roughly 375mm by 290mm when folded, the smallest of the standard newspaper sizes, generally associated with the more popular, less intellectual newspapers and having frequent negative connotations (see tabloid journalism).

■ Tabloid newspapers have a **readership** profile of largely C2, D and E social-class brackets and are read by those from a supervisory to a manual employment level.

■ Although their journalism is often inaccurate and sensationalised, tabloids increasingly have the power to dominate the national **agenda** and to influence the actions of politicians seeking to maintain their popularity.

■ *e.g. Daily Mirror, Star, Daily Express, Daily Mail, Sun*

■ *TIP* Tabloid-sized 'quality' newspapers like *The Times* and the *Independent* should not be seen as tabloid newspapers. They prefer the term **compact** to distinguish them from the more popular titles.

**tabloidisation:** the tendency of all media to follow the populist style of tabloid newspapers.

■ This involves the use of monosyllabic or simple vocabulary; attention-grabbing techniques such as alliteration or dramatic headlines or captions; simplified, personalised story lines or arguments that position the reader or viewer firmly on one side of an issue; the dramatisation and sensationalising of relatively trivial subjects.

**tabloid journalism:** the sensational, popular journalistic style of tabloid newspapers, often associated with irresponsibility and a low level of factual accuracy.

**take:** the sequence of film exposed by the starting and stopping of a film camera.

**talking heads:** television discussion programme in which the visual content is of people talking and in which an audience's attention is held largely through the dynamic of conversation.

■ *TIP* Talking heads are not regarded as visually interesting images.

**target audience:** the intended audience for a media product.

■ When producing a media text for mass consumption, identification of a target audience is essential so that media institutions can assess the likely response to the product and the investment risks involved.

■ The blockbuster movie *Titanic* (James Cameron, 1997) was carefully crafted to appeal to a range of audiences, with its generic mixture of disaster movie, historical reconstruction, action movie and romance. To this was added a hit-single theme song by Celine Dion. In spite of costing $200 million to produce, it grossed $1 billion at the box office, a record at the time.

■ *TIP* The target audience is not always the actual audience for a text, e.g. children under the age of 15 watching a 15- or 18-rated film when their parents are out.

**teaser:** a media device designed to attract and retain the attention of an audience in the hope that it will consume more of the product on offer.

■ In print media a teaser is a combination of words or phrases on a magazine cover or newspaper front page, designed to tease or entice the reader to buy the publication.

■ A teaser trailer is a short piece of film designed to entice audiences to view film and television productions.

■ On television news programmes teasers are brief announcements of stories yet to come, used to maintain audience interest.

**Technicolor:** a patented trademark for a technique of making films in colour, involving simultaneously exposing films sensitive to three different colours — red, blue and yellow — and then superimposing them to produce a full-colour print.

■ Technicolor was first developed as a three-colour process in 1932 and contracted to Disney for cartoons on a 3-year exclusive contract.

■ Technicolor films often produce exaggerated colour effects, e.g. *The Wizard of Oz* (Victor Fleming, 1939) and *Gone with the Wind* (Victor Fleming, 1939).

**teen movie:** a film directed at a target audience of teenagers and addressing specific teenage interests and experience in areas such as sexual identity, values and 'rights of passage' from school years into adulthood.

■ *e.g.* Teen movies include: 1950s classics such as *The Wild One* (Laslo Benedek, 1953), *Rebel without a Cause* (Nicholas Ray, 1955) and *Blackboard Jungle* (Richard Brooks, 1955); beach movies such as *Ride the Wild Surf* (Don Taylor, 1964); rock and roll and disco movies such as *American Graffiti* (George Lucas, 1973) and *Saturday Night Fever* (John Badham, 1977) and high-school movies such as *Clueless* (Amy Heckerling, 1995). Teen horror slasher movies such as *Scream*

(Wes Craven, 1996) are a variant, as is the alternative cult movie *Donnie Darko* (Richard Kelly, 2001).

**telefilm:** a feature-length film made for television.

***Telegraph:*** see *Daily Telegraph*.

**telephoto lense:** a lense with a long focal length, used to photograph and enlarge distant objects.

**text:** any constructed media product or piece of communication, whether print or audiovisual, which can be analysed and deconstructed.

**three-point lighting:** a lighting technique involving actors being lit from three points: a main source (or key light), a source filling shadows a (filler light) and a source backlighting the actors (a back light).

**thriller:** a film genre that aims to excite, disturb or frighten an audience by using narrative techniques of suspense and enigma followed by closure and resolution.

■ *e.g.* Alfred Hitchcock's *Spellbound* (1945), *Rear Window* (1954) and *Vertigo* (1958); *The Usual Suspects* (Bryan Singer, 1995)

**tilt:** a camera movement that involves moving the camera vertically up and down from a fixed position.

***Times, The:*** a quality daily compact newspaper.

■ Long viewed as the elitist voice of the English establishment, the 'thunderer', as it was once known, changed its style and politics because it was attracting too many readers of the wrong type. It became the newspaper flagship of Rupert Murdoch's News International in the UK after his acquisition of Times Newspapers (*The Times* and *The Sunday Times*) in 1981.

■ Murdoch's policy of moving publications down-market and to the political right has turned *The Times* into a populist quality paper, with a broader readership range and daily sales of 686,000 (January 2005).

**Time Warner (AOL/Time Warner):** an international media corporation formed by the merger of Time Inc. and Warner Brothers in 1990, and a subsequent merger with the internet company AOL in 2000. The company dropped the name AOL/Time Warner in 2003, when the AOL division suffered heavy losses and reverted to Time Warner

■ Operating on a global scale, Time Warner holdings include many familiar names including the following: *Time* magazine, Time Life books, Cable News Network, Atlantic and Elektra record labels, *Women's Own*, *Marie Claire*, *Ideal Home*, *Homes and Gardens* and Warner Brothers films. Time Warner took over IPC Media in 2001.

■ Time Warner is a major international player and a rival to the News Corporation.

**Todorov, Tzvetan (1939–):** a Bulgarian intellectual of the Russian formalist school, living and writing in France from the mid-1960s, author of a wide range of political and philosophical works.

■ He is particularly known for his work on 'narratology', or the structuring of narrative. His approach is founded on his belief in a common basis of human experience and the underlying narrative behind all human activity.

■ Todorov's sequence is made up of five propositions outlining a basic state of narration, which is disturbed and then re-established:
- a state of equilibrium where everything is in order
- a disruption of the order by an event
- a recognition that a disruption has taken place
- an attempt to repair the damage of the disruption
- a return to some kind of equilibrium

■ *e.g.* a history of the Second World War as narrative:
- equilibrium (stability or peace)
- force (a disruption of peace: Germany invades Poland)
- disequilibrium (climax: the war)
- force (in order to restore peace: Germany is defeated)
- equilibrium (peace on new terms or a form of compromise)

■ *TIP* It is easy to apply Todorov's pattern to **mainstream** film or television drama For example, in a disaster movie: the opening scenes show life before the disaster and engage the audience's interest in the characters; disaster occurs disrupting the characters' lives; key character figures or 'heroes' recognise the disaster and rush to the rescue; they struggle to repair the damage and save people's lives; calm and harmony are restored as all the characters come to terms with the past events. Audiences are reassured by the harmonious ending.

■ *TIP* Never try to force a narrative theory onto a structure or claim that the theory is proved by a structure. Use it as a tool, not a straightjacket.

**Touchstone Pictures:** a production company and subsidiary of the Walt Disney Company producing films not considered suitable for the Disney label.

■ *e.g. Pearl Harbor* (Michael Bay, 2001) classified in the USA as PG 13 for containing war-related violence, brief sensuality and profanity.

**tracking shot:** a camera shot in which the camera moves along rails to follow the subject.

■ When the rails are replaced by a moving platform on wheels, the shot is called a dolly shot.

**trailer:** a short teaser produced to advertise a new film.

■ Trailers are extracts from the production that have been edited together, often with added voice-over commentary. They are designed to provide a synoptic sample of the film's contents, together with the release date.

■ Trailers need to get a strong message across in a short time. They need to identify **genre** and to place the film in a recognisable context for a prospective audience. They also need to identify the core **narrative** without revealing the whole story line. They usually emphasise moments of high tension to grab the audience's attention. They highlight the roles and performances of key stars and the name of the director, with reference to previous successes. Above all, they need to emphasise the uniqueness and quality of the film in order to get it on an audience's 'must see' list.

■ Trailers are normally designed to be viewed by any audience and usually carry a U certificate, regardless of the category of the film they advertise.

**transmitter:** source of a telecommunications signal, such as radio.

■ The term is also used in some **process models** of mass communication to identify the origin of a media message.

**treatment:** the way in which a television or video product is to be approached in terms of **genre**, style, **iconography** and *mise en scène*.

■ A treatment would normally consist of a written description of how the intended product is to be styled and a basic outline of the action, as the first phase of the scriptwriting process.

**Trinity Mirror:** the UK's biggest newspaper publisher.

■ The group employs around 11,500 staff and produces some 250 titles. The company's varied media base includes national and regional newspapers, including the *Birmingham Post* and *Evening Mail*, websites and magazines. Nearly half the population reads one of its titles, which include the *Daily Mirror* (Mirror Group Newspapers), plus three of the top ten regional evening newspapers and three of the top ten regional Sunday newspapers.

**Twentieth Century Fox:** Hollywood studio created in 1935 during the **golden age** of Hollywood, now part of the **News Corporation** empire, owned by Rupert Murdoch.

**two-step flow:** a **passive audience** theory that sees media messages as reaching a mass audience in two stages.

■ The model was devised by Elihu Katz and Paul Lazarsfeld in 1955 and was a move away from the classic **stimulus response** principles, which had dominated audience theories during the 1940s.

■ The first of the two stages involves people called **opinion leaders** with influential status in society, who then pass on the message to the second stage, a larger audience. The mass audience's willingness to accept the message is seen as being influenced by the status of the opinion leader.

■ David Beckham's image is sought by advertisers in connection with mobile phone and sportswear sales since he is seen as an influential opinion leader with the youth target audience.

**typography:** the art or process of composing type and printing from it.

**UK Gold:** the most successful of the British satellite television channels, along with British Sky Broadcasting, operated by Flextech in conjunction with the British Broadcasting Corporation.

**uniform resource locator (URL):** an address that specifies the location of a file on the internet.

■ *e.g.* www.google.co.uk

**United Business Media (formerly United Newspapers, United News and Media and United MAI):** a media company associated with Lord Hollick, with 35% holdings in Five (formerly Channel 5) and ownership of other high-tech publishing and business services.

■ The company was formerly a stakeholder in regional Independent Television franchises (e.g. Yorkshire, Tyne Tees and Anglia), part owner of Independent Television News and also owner of Express Newspapers, which it sold to Richard Desmond's Northern and Shell company in 1997.

■ The company sold its ITV holdings to Granada in 2000 and has since consolidated its activities in the production of business information services.

**United MAI:** company name of United News and Media following 1996 merger with the television company MAI, later changed to United Business Media.

**United News and Media:** company name of United Newspapers from 1995 to 1996.

**United Newspapers:** a British newspaper and magazine publishing company founded in 1918.

■ United Newspapers built up a considerable stake in regional newspaper titles by the 1970s and in 1985 the company bought Express Newspapers. In 1995 it changed its name to United News and Media to reflect its wider media holdings and in 1996 the company merged with Lord Hollick's television and finance-based MAI and became United MAI.

**Universal:** a film production company founded as Universal Studios in 1922; part of Vivendi Universal from 2000.

■ Universal was always smaller than the giant Hollywood studios.

■ In 1995, it was acquired by Seagram. Its operations expanded in the global market, with its acquisition of PolyGram music in 1998, making the Universal Music Group the world's largest music company.

■ It was bought by the French company Vivendi Canal Plus in 2000 to create Vivendi Universal, a major global media organisation.

**URL:** see uniform resource locator.

**uses and gratifications theory:** an active audience theory, developed by Jay Blumler and Elihu Katz (1975), that focuses on 'what people do with the media' rather than what the media does to people, arguing that audiences are free to pick and choose from a wide range of media products to satisfy their own needs.

■ Individuals may seek: diversion in the form of escape from reality, emotional release or pleasure; personal relationships through companionship and sociability, using knowledge of television characters to interact with others; personal identity and a sense of self through identifying as members of a particular audience; surveillance through finding out about the world and the events that affect them.

■ *TIP* Although useful as an active theory, it assumes that audience needs are identified and met by the media and underestimates the media's role in generating those needs in the first place.

**utopia:** an idealised (often future) world where everything is perfect, derived from the title of a book by Sir Thomas More (1478–1535) which described an island where people live in social harmony ruled by a perfect government.

■ The term 'utopian solution' is used by the genre theorist Richard Dyer (1977) to describe the appeal of escapist film genres, such as Westerns, to audiences. Dyer sees these genres as offering a kind of fantasy escapism from everyday problems and routines.

**value judgement:** a subjective opinion based on an individual's attitudes, beliefs and values rather than on any objective criteria.

**vamp:** term for a sexually alluring actress, created during the silent movie era by William Fox (1879–1952).

■ Vamps were openly sexual and erotic and provided a strong contrast to the ideal of innocence represented by stars such as Mary Pickford.

■ *e.g.* Theda Bara in *A Fool There Was* (Frank Powell, 1914) and *Cleopatra* (J. Gordon Edwards, 1917)

**vampire movie:** a subgenre of horror in which the subject matter is loosely based on characters from Bram Stoker's novel *Dracula* (1897).

■ The first vampire movie was F. W. Murnau's *Nosferatu* (1922), with a screenplay based loosely on the original Stoker novel. Count Dracula (Orlock), the vampire and creature of the night, inhabits an ancient castle in Transylvania. Overcome by the beauty of a portrait of a guest's wife, he seeks to establish himself in western Europe bringing with him plague and unexpected death. He is finally overcome through the entrapment of a virtuous woman, the object of his desire, who holds him until daybreak when he is destroyed by the sun.

■ Vampire iconography includes mysterious gothic castles, blood, vampire teeth, graveyards, crucifixes, stakes, coffins, bats, virgins, werewolves, wild natural settings and vampire hunters.

■ The vampire genre has proved versatile and adaptable to social change and changes in audience expectation, with variants reflecting fear of disease, the AIDS crisis and with subtexts relating to homosexuality and fear of sexual excess.

■ *e.g.* *Dracula* (Tod Browning, 1931), *Nosferatu* (homage movie by Werner Herzog, 1979), *Bram Stoker's Dracula* (tribute movie, Francis Ford Coppola, 1992), *Interview with the Vampire* (Neil Jordan, 1994), *Blade* (Stephen Norrington, 1998), *Underworld* (Len Wiseman, 2003)

**verisimilitude:** seeming to be like or to be connected to the real.

■ The term is important in many media **genres** because it determines the level of audience engagement and willingness to engage in **suspension of disbelief.**

■ *TIP* Contemporary war films need to convey a sense of verisimilitude to be credible. Reconstructions of Second World War battle scenes, with special-effects bullets flying around the heads of the actors, are now seen as more real than newsreel footage of the actual events, e.g. *Saving Private Ryan* (Steven Spielberg, 1998).

**vertical integration:** the merger or takeover of companies operating at different stages of the production/distribution process.

■ Total vertical integration gives a company control of a product from raw materials to distribution.

■ *e.g.* In media industries, the takeover by a newspaper owner of a distribution service and retail outlets such as newsagents would be vertical integration.

**Viacom:** a media corporation, owner of Paramount, CBS (Columbia Broadcasting System), **MTV** and Blockbuster Video, together with television and radio stations and advertising holdings in the USA.

**video diary:** a record of everyday events, feelings and experiences recorded on a video camera set up by and then focused on the individual concerned.

■ The subject looks into the camera and describes his/her experiences as if writing a personal diary.

■ Reality television programmes often use video-diary techniques to record the private thoughts of individuals taking part in group activities.

**video game:** any game designed to be played on a home computer system, such as *Nintendo* and *Sony Playstation*.

■ Increasingly sophisticated, these games generate a whole range of virtual characters which in many cases are developed into feature films, e.g. Lara Croft and *Tomb Raider* (Simon West, 2001). The relationship also works in reverse with games being generated by characters drawn from books and films, e.g. the *Harry Potter* series and *The Lord of the Rings*.

■ *TIP* Violence in video games has led to concerns over their availability to children and teenagers, particularly after claims that the young killers in the April 1999 Columbine High School massacre in Colorado, USA, in which 14 people died, had been influenced by the game 'Doom'. The **BBFC** classifies some games under its remit in the UK, but a self-regulatory system also operates to attempt to ensure that particularly violent games do not get into the hands of young people.

**video nasty:** a video with a high level of violence or sexual violence as its principal content.

■ Video nasties became the centre of a media **effects theory** debate in the early 1990s following the murder of toddler Jamie Bulger by two 10-year-old boys said to have been influenced by watching a video of the film *Child's Play 3* (Jack Bender, 1991). Although this film was not a video nasty, and there was no evidence that the boys had even watched it, a successful campaign was launched by **right-wing** newspapers, including the *Daily Mail*, to introduce legislation to restrict, ban or tightly classify all potentially offending material.

■ *e.g.* *The Texas Chainsaw Massacre* (Tobe Hooper, 1974), *I Spit on Your Grave* (Meir Zarchi, 1978), *The Driller Killer* (Abel Ferrara, 1979)

**Video Recordings Act of 1984:** an Act of parliament requiring all films on video to be certified for release by the **British Board of Film Classification.**

■ The Act was introduced in response to **moral panic** over the contents of videos and their potential influence on behaviour following the murder of the toddler Jamie Bulger.

**Vivendi Universal:** a global media and communications conglomerate, with holdings in publishing, telecommunications, television, film, music and the internet.

■ Vivendi Universal was formed by the merger of Vivendi Canal Plus with Seagram (Universal Studios) in 2000.

***Vogue*:** an internationally famous 'glossy' fashion magazine, published in various national editions by **Condé Nast.**

■ *Vogue* is particularly known for the quality of its fashion photography, involving top models and photographers.

**voice-over:** the dubbing of an actor's voice over a film or video production.

**voyeur:** a person who watches the behaviour of others without their knowledge from a detached, non-involved position and for reasons of self-gratification.

**vox pop (from the Latin *vox populi,* 'the voice of the people'):** in broadcasting, a short interview conducted to record the opinion of ordinary people and to create a sense of engagement and involvement for the viewer or listener.

**war movie:** a film genre in which the action takes place during a war.

- War movies usually focus on twentieth- and twenty-first century wars and the narratives often involve ethical and moral positioning in relation to the conflict.
- Classic First World War war films such as *La Grande Illusion* (Jean Renoir, 1937) and *All Quiet on the Western Front* (Lewis Milestone, 1930) carried pacifist messages.
- During the Second World War, British studios produced a whole series of patriotic films designed to boost morale in support of the conflict, e.g. *Dangerous Moonlight* (Brian Desmond Hurst, 1941). In the 1950s the mood was one of British triumphalism after victory, e.g. *The Dam Busters* (Michael Anderson, 1955) and *Cockleshell Heroes* (José Ferrer, 1955).
- In the face of domestic anti-war feeling, the Vietnam War film *The Green Berets* (John Wayne and Ray Kellogg, 1968) encouraged a pro-US patriotic view of war. Other Vietnam War films, such as *Apocalypse Now* (Francis Ford Coppola, 1976) and *Full Metal Jacket* (Stanley Kubrick, 1987), represent the horrific and dehumanising aspects of that conflict.
- With increased emphasis on the holocaust and the moral justification for the Second World War, a film like *Saving Private Ryan* (Steven Spielberg, 1998) works on a **fabulation** level, created 55 years after the events and emphasising the moral superiority of US values over those of Nazi Germany.
- *Black Hawk Down* (Ridley Scott, 2001) covered a specific event in the Somalia conflict of the early 1990s and encouraged a pro-US patriotic view of interventionist war. It was used as moral justification by the pro-war camp in the Iraq conflict (2003).

**Warner Brothers:** a Hollywood film company founded in 1923, merged with Time Inc. in 1990 to form **Time Warner**, with Turner Broadcasting in 1996, and with AOL in 2000 to create the conglomerate **AOL/Time Warner**, one of the largest global media corporations.

- *e.g.* Classic Warner Brothers productions include: *The Jazz Singer* (Alan Crosland, 1927) and *Bonnie and Clyde* (Arthur Penn, 1967).

**Watergate:** the name of a hotel and office complex in Washington and the campaign headquarters for the Democratic Party in 1972.

■ The offices were bugged on the orders of President Richard Nixon. The subsequent exposure by *Washington Post* reporters Bob Woodward and Carl Bernstein of the bugging, and of the deceit and corruption involved in the attempted cover-up, caused a major national scandal, which eventually lead to the resignation of Nixon in 1974.

■ The case is often cited as a prime example of the power of a free press.

■ The impact of the scandal was such that the suffix 'gate' has been attached by journalists to many other, often less important scandals and disputes, as a way of making them seem more significant than they often are, e.g. Irangate (1987), the secret selling of arms to Iran by President Reagan; Camillagate (1992), the scandal resulting from the release of taped intimate telephone conversations between Prince Charles and the then Camilla Parker-Bowles; Zippergate (2000), the scandal of President Clinton's relationship with Monica Lewinsky.

**watershed:** the divide between early and late evening television viewing, set at 9 p.m. and used as a marker to monitor and control the content of programmes with regard to sex, violence and bad language.

■ Early evening programmes are assumed to be family viewing while later evening viewing is seen as adult.

■ *TIP* The existence of video and DVD recorders, the presence of televisions in children's bedrooms and access to the internet raise questions as to the relevance of the concept in a multimedia, multichannel environment.

**webcam:** a real-time video camera that sends digital images to a web server, continuously or at regular intervals, for viewing on the internet.

■ Webcams have a range of uses, including in chat rooms, for video conferencing and to provide traffic information.

**website:** a related collection of internet web files located on the same server and accessible via a browser through a unique address 24 hours a day.

■ Websites include a homepage — the first file visitors see — which explains what the site contains and how to navigate it. All files usually contain hyperlinks to allow movement within the site or to other sites.

**Western:** a film genre based on the developmental history of the USA, set in the Wild West.

■ Westerns have a distinctive range of iconographical elements, stock characters and plot options representing the aspirations and conflicts arising from the growth and development of America.

■ Archetypal characters include cowboys, Native American Indians, sheriffs, preachers, bar keepers, schoolma'ams, saloon women, gunfighters, ranchers, quack doctors, old timers and store keepers.

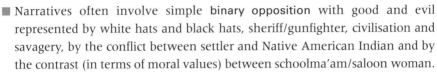

- Narratives often involve simple **binary opposition** with good and evil represented by white hats and black hats, sheriff/gunfighter, civilisation and savagery, by the conflict between settler and Native American Indian and by the contrast (in terms of moral values) between schoolma'am/saloon woman.
- *e.g.* Classic Westerns: *Stagecoach* (John Ford, 1939), *Shane* (George Steven, 1953), *Rio Bravo* (Howard Hawks, 1959). Over 70 years, the genre has seen many variations and has often been used in a **fabulation** sense to explore moral conflict and social changes, e.g. racism in *The Searchers* (John Ford, 1956) and the corrupting effect of violence in *Unforgiven* (Clint Eastwood, 1992). It became heavily stylised and anti-heroic in the spaghetti Western, e.g. *The Good, the Bad and the Ugly* (Sergio Leone, 1966) and in satirical parody, e.g. *Blazing Saddles* (Mel Brooks, 1974). With the crisis of US values during the Vietnam War came the anti-army *Soldier Blue* (Ralph Nelson, 1970) and *Little Big Man* (Arthur Penn, 1970), while with the revision of US history and increasing respect for Native Americans and their lifestyle came *Dances with Wolves* (Kevin Costner, 1990).

**white balance:** the setting of a video camera to match a particular source of light in order to ensure picture quality.

**Whitehouse, Mary (1910–2001):** a populist campaigner against sex and violence on television.

- Styling herself as an ordinary housewife, Whitehouse launched a 'Clean up TV' campaign in the early 1960s. This was at a time when the **British Broadcasting Corporation**, in particular, was experimenting with fresh new programme styles and reaching a younger audience with a more open approach towards sex and relationships (e.g. *The Wednesday Play* series) and an irreverent approach toward politicians.
- Whitehouse became a national figure for her outspoken attacks on the BBC. Her assertions that television was a growing threat to family life were never substantiated by meaningful evidence and she often boasted of not having seen the material she condemned.
- Together with the Catholic peer Lord Longford, she began the Festival of Light, a **right-wing** religious movement and **pressure group** opposing sexually explicit imagery and advocating a return to traditional **family values**.
- Whitehouse founded the television pressure group the **National Viewers and Listeners Association** in 1965 and monitored film and television productions in a random fashion for whatever she found shocking and offensive.
- Films she attacked included *Last Tango in Paris* (Bernardo Bertolucci, 1972), *Themroc* (Claude Faraldo, 1972) and *The Exorcist* (William Friedkin, 1973). Her campaign against **video nasties** influenced government legislation and she successfully prosecuted the journal *Gay News* under the ancient law of blasphemy. Her pressure group helped to generate **moral panic**, with

considerable support from the press, and had some influence on public policy, particularly under Conservative governments until 1997.

■ Although her views were reactionary and she believed in heavy censorship, Whitehouse established the important principle of accountability in broadcasting.

**white space:** deliberately blank spaces on printed pages of a magazine or newspaper, designed as part of the overall appearance and design.

**wipe:** a moving image editing technique that involves one image wiping another off the screen.

**witch hunt:** a term sometimes used to describe the media's vindictive persecution of an individual or group targeted because of some perceived offence or misdemeanor.

■ The idea carries the sense that, once having found someone to accuse, the media will seek out and pursue others and in doing so encourage moral panic.

**women's magazines:** lifestyle magazines with a principal target audience of women.

■ Women's magazines have been subject to extensive studies in terms of content analysis and are often seen as reflecting stereotypical representations of women.

■ They can also be important markers for issues affecting and concerning women, and their changing content over the last 50 years can be seen as an indicator of the changing role of women in society.

**World Wide Web (www):** the international computer network and information retrieval system that provides global access, via web browsers and through the use of hypertext transfer protocol, to web pages on the internet.

■ Web pages may be in graphic, video, or audio format.

**wrap:** the end of a day's shoot in the film industry.

■ The term can also mean the movement of a news item from studio bulletin to reporter, to film clip, back to reporter and then back to bulletin reader.

**www:** see World Wide Web.

**X certificate:** classification of a film with adult content, introduced in 1951, to be viewed only by those over 16 under the **British Board of Film Censors** classification system.

■ With the increase in representations of sex and violence in mainstream cinema, the age restriction was raised to 18 in 1970 and replaced by the 18 certificate category in 1982.

**xenophobia:** a dislike or fear of foreigners.

■ Generating fear of foreigners through the use of **stereotypes** has been a common practice in the media, particularly the tabloid press, as a means of creating a consensus around an issue and influencing public opinion.

■ *e.g.* Before the First World War, the *Daily Mail* ran an anti-German campaign, suggesting that Germany was threatening the British Empire and thereby preparing public opinion for the coming war. More recently, the terms 'Brussels' and 'Europe' have been used in an anti-European, derogatory sense to suggest a threat to British independence. The term 'bogus asylum seeker' has also been used in a derogatory sense to suggest illegal immigrants, who are seen as posing an unspecified threat.

**youth culture:** any of a range of youth subcultures from the 1950s through to the present day, including aspects of dress, behaviour, music preferences and relationships.

■ Youth cultures have been largely defined and exploited by advertising and marketing agencies as a means of identifying audiences and markets of young people with a high level of spending power. Youth culture groups have often been associated with 'cult' media texts and actors with whom they can identify.

■ *e.g.* Teddyboys (1950s) identified with *Rock around the Clock* (Fred F. Sears, 1956), *Rebel without a Cause* (Nicholas Ray, 1955) and *The Wild One* (Laslo Benedek, 1953). Mods (1960s) identified with *Tommy* (The Who/Ken Russell, 1975). The late 1950s and 1960s saw the Beat Generation influenced by the

novels of Jack Kerouac, e.g. *On the Road*, while 1960s **counterculture** admired *Easy Rider* (Dennis Hopper, 1969). Skinheads (1960s–90s) had *A Clockwork Orange* (Stanley Kubrick, 1971) and *Romper Stomper* (Geoffrey Wright, 1992), and punks a cult stage and film musical production with *The Rocky Horror Show* (1970s). The contemporary cult movie *Donnie Darko* (Richard Kelly, 2001) appeals to moshers. Goths have always celebrated **horror** movies, e.g. *Interview with the Vampire* (Neil Jordan, 1994).

**zapping:** the practice of rapid television-channel hopping, using a zapper or television remote-control handset.

■ Zapping results from a large number of television channels showing broadly similar programmes, which do not retain the interest of the viewer. It reflects an increasingly low concentration span among viewers where viewing habits do not involve watching whole programmes from start to finish.

■ Zapping works against the intentions of television schedulers who attempt to grab and hold an audience for an evening's viewing.

**Zip:** a television company specialising in interactive advertising which allows the viewer to participate interactively with the advertisements.

■ *e.g.* A campaign for *Bridget Jones: the Edge of Reason* (Beeban Kidron, 2004), was designed to generate viewer interest before the film's launch. Viewers were able to watch clips from the film, take part in a profile quiz to see if they were like Bridget, enter a competition and see 'behind-the-scenes' footage from the film. A campaign for Honda allowed viewers to record their own voices and hear them within the advertisement.

■ *TIP* Zip would like to develop an interactive advertising television channel.

**zombie movie:** a horror **subgenre** in which the living are plagued by armies of the living dead who usually survive by devouring the living.

■ Although the narratives seem fairly simple, the genre does reflect a disturbing underlying fear of disease and infection, with the healthy slaughtering the zombie armies to avoid contamination.

■ *e.g.* *Night of the Living Dead* (George Romero, 1968), *Dawn of the Dead* (George Romero, 1979), *Dawn of the Dead* remake (Zak Snyder, 2004)

■ *TIP* Zombie movies mutate into other forms. *28 Days Later* (Danny Boyle, 2002) leans heavily on zombie iconography with its armies of plague-ridden deranged creatures seeking to infect the healthy. The **hybrid** genre movie *From Dusk Till Dawn* (Robert Rodriguez, 1996) has zombie characters mixed in with vampires.

**zoom:** the adjustment of a camera lens to allow the operator progressively to move in close or to pull away from the subject.